FIGHTER PILOT PARENT

LEADING YOUR KIDS WITH LESSONS FROM THE COCKPIT

BRAD "BRICK" CONNERS,
CAPTAIN, US NAVY, RETIRED

RIVER GROVE
BOOKS

JENNELYN
FAITH, FAMILY, FRIENDS, & FUN
CHECK 6
BRICK

This publication is designed to provide accurate and authoritative information in regard to the subject matter covered. It is sold with the understanding that the publisher and author are not engaged in rendering legal, accounting, or other professional services. Nothing herein shall create an attorney-client relationship, and nothing herein shall constitute legal advice or a solicitation to offer legal advice. If legal advice or other expert assistance is required, the services of a competent professional should be sought.

Published by River Grove Books
Austin, TX
www.rivergrovebooks.com

For permission to reprint prayer by CDR John J. "Bug" Roach, III, grateful acknowledgment is made to The Tailhook Association. Tailhook.net.

Distributed by River Grove Books

Design and composition by Greenleaf Book Group and Kim Lance
Cover design by Greenleaf Book Group and Kim Lance

Publisher's Cataloging-in-Publication data is available.

Print ISBN: 978-1-63299-229-1

eBook ISBN: 978-1-63299-230-7

First Edition

This book is dedicated to my family—Terrie, Sarah, Rachel, Anna, and Bradford; to the men and women of the VFA-151 Vigilantes; and to the men and women of Naval Base Ventura County.

Every night, our kids knew that mistakes were in the past, opportunity was in the future, and that their parents, brothers, and sisters were the best wingmen they would ever have.

Prayer written by
Commander John J."Bug" Roach, III, USN
1944–1991

———

LORD, WE ARE THE NATION! We celebrate our birthday on July 4th, 1776, with the Declaration of Independence as our birth certificate. The bloodlines of the world run in our veins, because we offer freedom and liberty to all whom are oppressed. We are many things and many people. We are the nation.

We sprawl from the Atlantic to the Pacific, to Alaska and Hawaii. Three million square miles throbbing with industry and with life. We are the forest, field, mountain, and desert. We are the wheat fields of Kansas, the granite hills of Vermont, and the snowcapped peaks of the Sierra Nevada. We are the Brooklyn Bridge, we are the grain elevators in the Farm Belt. We are the Golden Gate. We are the nation.

We are 213 million living souls, and yet we are the ghosts of millions who have lived and died for us. We are Nathan Hale and Paul Revere. We are Washington, Jefferson, and Patrick Henry. We are Lee, Grant, Abe Lincoln, and George Bush. We are the famous and the unknown. We are presidents, we are paupers. We are the nation.

We stood at Lexington and fired the shot heard around the world. We remember the Alamo, the *Maine*, Pearl Harbor, Inchon, and the Persian Gulf. When freedom calls, we answer. We left our heroic dead at Belleau Wood, on the rock of Corregidor, on the bleak slopes of Korea, in the steaming jungles of Vietnam, and under the rubble of Beirut. We are the nation.

We are schools and colleges, churches and synagogues. We are a ballot dropped in a box, the harmonious voice of a choir in a cathedral, the crack of a bat, and the roar of a crowd in a stadium. We are craftsmen, teachers, businessmen, and judges. We are laborers and nurses. We are parents and we are children. We are soldiers, sailors, and airmen. We are peaceful villages, small towns, and cities that never sleep. Yes, we are the nation, and these are the things that we are.

We were conceived in freedom, and dear God, if you are willing, in freedom we will spend the rest of our days. May we always be thankful for the blessings you have bestowed upon us. May we be humble to the less fortunate and assist those in need. May we never forget the continuing cost of freedom. May we always remember that if we are to remain the land of the free, we must continue always to be the home of the brave. May our wishbone never be found where our backbone should be. May we possess always, the integrity, the courage, and the strength to keep ourselves unshackled, to remain always a citadel of freedom and a beacon of hope to the world.

We are the nation.
This is our wish.
This is our hope.
And this is our prayer.

Amen

CONTENTS

AIRCRAFT CARRIER: A DAY IN THE LIFE

———

It is said that a US Navy fighter aircraft is airborne somewhere in the world every second of every day, promoting peace and prosperity, protecting national and global interests, and if necessary, projecting power or rendering disaster relief.

In order to accomplish this amazing feat, the United States deploys eleven special ships, called aircraft carriers, strategically around the globe. They are a marvel in engineering; they are a marvel in self-sufficiency; and they are a marvel in conducting aircraft operations. When a global crisis of any type strikes, the first question that often gets asked is: "Where are the carriers?"

If you have ever stood or floated next to one, you know how intimidating they are. They are mammoth. At over 1,100 feet long, it is just 150 feet short of the Empire State Building. A football or soccer game could be played across its width, and it stands twenty stories high *above* the waterline. The United States' carriers are surprisingly fast thanks to two nuclear reactors spinning four gigantic thirty-ton propellers, and are also fairly maneuverable despite their size. And other than for food, aviation fuel, and weapons, they are mostly self-sufficient.

Of course, this 100,000-ton marvel gets much smaller the moment you try to take off and land from it. For takeoff (or launch), an aircraft's front wheel strut is connected to one of the ship's four catapults. Then, in the span of 300 feet and two seconds, the catapult accelerates a high-performance jet to 150 miles per hour, and *poof*—you're flying. Disney's California Screamin' roller coaster, now the Incredicoaster, is about as close to the real experience as you can find. To land, that same aircraft uses a hook lowered from its back end to "snatch" one of the four cables stretched across a 75-foot-wide, 766-foot-long landing area. Most runways you are probably used to landing on are 10,000 feet long and 200 feet wide. The cable unwinds at such a precise rate that it can bring a 35,000-pound jet going 160 miles per hour to a complete stop in less than three seconds—without ripping the hook out of the airplane! Other than slamming on your car's brakes in an emergency at a terrifically high speed, it's tough to find an equivalent experience in normal life. And when day gives way to night or clear skies turn dark and cloudy, the ship begins to shrink in relative size for any pilot trying to land on what now looks like a floating harmonica.

So how do fighter pilots get the ship back to manageable size for landing? There is a secret something that is often overlooked by those who tend to only marvel at its technical might and jaw-dropping size. This singular, extraordinary secret provides the decisive advantage for a pilot in every situation, every undertaking, and every mission. There is only one thing that can restore the ship back to a manageable size to make it possible for the pilot to land. What is this secret something? It is the carrier's crew—its family, if you will.

Each member of this 5,000-person family acts in synchronous harmony. The captain and commanders set the course, prepare and integrate their teams, and make extremely difficult risk decisions. Every other member of this special family has a unique role and function.

They work in a perpetual cycle of survival. If they are not learning, they are teaching or doing. And if they are not being led, they are leading. This time-honored system accelerates the progression and mastery of the crucial skills they must acquire for the carrier to operate at the highest of standards. On the carrier flight deck, teams are distinguished by the color of the jersey, helmet, or floatation vest they wear: red, white, green, blue, purple, or yellow. Ordnance teams (in red) are building, moving, testing, and loading weapons. White clothing signifies a safety team who tend to be the risk referees and supervisors who are integrated into both routine (launch and recovery) and special evolutions (like aircraft emergencies). Maintenance personnel wear green. The newest and most vulnerable family members wear blue, so the rest of the team can keep an eye on them as they learn how to survive on the most dangerous four-and-a-half acres of real estate known to aviation. Fuelers wear purple, and those who direct, move, launch, and recover aircraft wear yellow. This entire team brings the ship to life, gives it personality and character, and allows the extraordinary to appear routine and ordinary.

Some facts may astound you. Elsewhere on the ship, it's almost impossible to tell if it is day or night since there are no windows. Office and work spaces are mostly small and depend on fluorescent lights for illumination. One of the best parts about flying or working on the flight deck is that you get to see the sun. Each day, 16,000 meals are prepared in seven galleys (kitchens), and it is not uncommon to go through 1,600 pounds of chicken, 160 gallons of milk, 30 cases of cereal, and 350 pounds of lettuce on any given day. Supply ships (grocery stores) deliver almost a million pounds of food every ten days. And just like most families, those with birthdays are treated to a special meal complete with a tablecloth, a wine glass (no wine), and nice music.

This special family comes from all walks of life, all states of the union, all ethnic groups, and it is rich in diversity. Still, there are two things that are common to them all. The first is not letting their ship-mates down, and the second is that they all count the number of days until they will be reunited with their real families or friends.

It is my hope that this preface to *Fighter Pilot Parent* will give you a better understanding and context for the experiences I'm about to share with you and the lessons that I have drawn from them—both as a pilot and as a parent. I've mentioned family quite a bit and for good reason. For many who volunteer to serve, the Navy, their squadron, and their ship are often the only family they have ever known. And the Navy takes great pride in giving them a world-class substitute.

BEST TRAINED, MOST FEARED

The world is a wonderful and amazing place. It is full of hope, opportunity, purpose, and beauty. That's the upside. But always lurking close by, and often interleaved inseparably with the wonderful, you'll find the other world: a world of danger, risk, evil, and darkness. The challenge in life, of course, is to successfully navigate between the two, and when you get off track, to quickly correct back to safety.

The Edge of the Envelope

As a parent, have you ever been anxious about your child venturing away from the safety and security of home? If you're like most responsible parents, I'll assume you answered yes without much thought or deliberation. Your anxiety levels may have spiked just thinking about it. After all, it's a dangerous and hostile world out there. Now, let me ask you one more question: Would you believe that your anxiety level and concerns are not that much different than those of a strike fighter squadron commander launching his newest pilot into combat for the first time?

It seems to me that in life, and especially when you are flying a high-performance jet, the greatest opportunities exist precisely at the same place you find the greatest risk—at the edge of the envelope, as we say in aviation—the place between glory and humiliating defeat. In sports, it's called being in "the zone." Jazz musicians call it "having chops." It is that special place where creativity and skill mastery are bound by the laws of nature. Fighter pilots are trained and expected to successfully perform right there, at that sweet spot, all the time. If they fail to get close to it, they will underperform and expose themselves—and their team—to a variety of potential risks or, even worse, mission failure. If they go too far beyond it, the risks tend to be much worse; sometimes there is no recovery and things can turn catastrophic. I have often felt this way with regard to my kids when trying as a parent to determine how hard to push and how much to protect.

Being a fighter pilot is not just about mastering complex skills. It is a way of life where faith, character, integrity, leadership, patriotism, managing fear, teaching, and learning are combined in such a unique way that ordinary people (like me) can be transformed into individuals capable of extraordinary sacrifice, skill, and service. Fighter pilots are certainly not alone; many professional communities place a premium on peak personal performance, quick thinking, discipline, integrity, and character—and for these I have the greatest respect. But when you add in high-speed, g-forces, and night carrier landings, do overs are far and few between for the fighter pilots. There are no shortcuts, and there is no faking it.

US Navy fighter pilots prepare for high-risk environments in very specific ways, and their leaders develop unique capabilities and attributes in their subordinates the same way. Their methods would never be a bad model to emulate for any high-risk enterprise or endeavor. And that includes parenting, in my opinion.

President John F. Kennedy was quoted as saying: "The ancient Greek definition of happiness was the full use of your powers along lines of excellence." He also said, "There are risks and costs to a program of action. But they are far less than the long-range risks and costs of comfortable inaction." This book outlines a program of action where happiness is plotted against your full use of powers along lines of excellence.

As both a parent and a former Navy F/A-18 Hornet Squadron commander, I can attest that there is no real significant emotional difference in the way I feel about each of these roles. As a parent, I want my kids to be healthy, successful, and safe. I want them to return home in one piece, but with valuable experiences that will continue to add value to their lives. As a squadron commander, I rated my success on those exact same things. Fortunately for US fighter pilots, there are proven processes in place that always produce a very high first-time success rate.

For parents, those processes are not so clear or easy.

Unconditional Love and the Task at Hand

The two most sobering and simultaneously joyful moments in my life were the birth of my first daughter and the day I accepted command of a Navy F/A-18 Strike Fighter Squadron.

With my daughter, my objectives were pretty simple: to guide her to become an educated, high-character adult who is socially astute and ready for a scary world—with a dash of boy aversion until age thirty. For the pilots in my squadron, my objectives were equally simple—to make them the best trained and most feared pilots in the sky.

For both my daughter and my squadron, unconditional love was instantaneous. That love immediately compelled me to do everything in my power to protect them from, and prepare them for, any and all threats they might face. For both, I was worried that I wasn't qualified for the task at hand.

Identifying objectives is easy. Accomplishing them is the hard part. With pilots, at least there is a self-selection process that delivers a relatively trained and proficient combat-ready aviator who meets the minimal requirements. With kids, however, you own the entire development cycle. They don't come with instruction manuals. How *could* there be one? God made each one of them perfect—and *unique*. You and you alone have to figure out the best plan for each kid. Ask any parent of multiple children, and they will tell you that despite having the same parents, the same environment, and the same love and nurturing, they all turn out radically different (the Hanson brothers from the movie *Slap Shot* aside). My four kids tend to validate this theory. Not surprisingly, pilots also have a pretty wide personality distribution too. They learn differently. They handle stress differently. They perform differently.

So how do you get your kids to that best trained, most feared status? Ultimately, you want them to enjoy a high rate of first-time success in every phase of their life. Well, at the risk of destroying every myth and perception you may have about the Navy fighter community, and assuming the movie *Top Gun* is your basis of understanding it, I am about to share with you how my experiences helped shape and influence me as a parent—as imperfect and ordinary as I may be in that role.

Commit to the Chase

We all screw up. We all make mistakes. There is no such thing as a perfect parent or a perfect fighter pilot. Even the great football coach Vince Lombardi observed, "Perfection is not attainable, but if we chase perfection, we can catch excellence."

So there it is, the first and most important lesson: Be committed to the chase. If you can't adapt to changing environments, if you can't invest in continuous learning, if you can't admit to mistakes, if you can't muster the courage to make hard decisions, and if you can't be disciplined in executing the plan with character and integrity, the chase is over before it starts. I've screwed up as a pilot, a parent, a husband, and a coach. We all screw up, but the good pilots and the good parents learn from their mistakes.

When flying with brand-new pilots (we call them "nuggets"), I would always tell them, to their amazement and surprise, "I am counting on you to save my life." Wow! That's very serious stuff for the most junior pilots in a squadron. I told them that they, and they alone, would have access to exclusive life-and-death cockpit information that their Flight Lead (myself) would not be privy to, and therefore, they must have the courage and confidence to take action on their own. I then shared with them that I had *never* flown the perfect mission—ever. But I had come close many times.

I told them that although I strived and prepared to be perfect on each mission, I always made mistakes. And in that crucial moment with my newest pilots, I created a binding contract that we would cover each other's backs—regardless of our experience or knowledge. After that eyepopper, I would always add that my mistakes had continued to get smaller and less frequent over time—and that's what chasing perfection and catching excellence means.

Written in Blood

In naval aviation, we have a system of describing and highlighting the seriousness of a flight-related problem. In our *Flying for Dummies* publications, you'll find NOTES, WARNINGS, and CAUTIONS bold-faced in the text. A note implies a suboptimal system performance. A caution implies risk of injury or system failure. And a warning, as you might have guessed, implies risk of death or catastrophic system failure. Most, if not all, notes, warnings, and cautions were written in blood. That is to say, someone had to suffer so that others might benefit. Two themes are evident here: We can and should learn a lot from others, and there are certain mistakes that are unrecoverable. As parents, those are the mistakes we must avoid at all costs. I will try to convey the parent version of NOTES, WARNINGS, and CAUTIONS in the passages that follow.

★★★

As a young pilot, I was training to be a landing signal officer (LSO). An LSO is a pilot who, in addition to flying, talks airplanes down as they're landing on an aircraft carrier. In that line of work, a ramp strike is the worst possible thing that could happen. A ramp strike occurs when an aircraft lands short of the landing area and crashes into the back end of the ship (the ramp or round down), which in most cases results in fire, injury, and death.

One day I had the very good fortune of being trained by the legend of Navy LSOs—a gentleman with the famous nickname "Bug." John J. "Bug" Roach, III is often said to have been the Michael Jordan, the Wayne Gretzky, or even the Brett Favre of LSOs. Take your pick: He has saved countless lives simply by "talking" them down and aboard. At that point in my career, he was the guy they sent to any aircraft carrier when it was having significant problems with landing performance. Finding the courage, I finally asked Bug if he had ever "waved" (the term we LSOs use to describe controlling a landing aircraft) a ramp strike. To my surprise, he answered, "Sure, lots."

What? How could that be? He was the master. His response to my obvious surprise was profound. He explained that there are times when the pilot or aircraft will do something so dangerous and so quick that it is beyond anyone's ability to control or correct—and that action is instantaneously unrecoverable. You just run out of options. He finished with, "If you do this long enough and often enough, you'll know exactly what I'm talking about."[1]

> "The only known way to avoid crashing airplanes is to never fly them. And the only known way to raise a perfect and totally successful kid is to never have one."

Sadly, even the best squadron commanders, the best fighter pilots, the best LSOs, and the best parents fail occasionally. It's all about managing risk in a high-risk venture. You really can't totally control all of it. The only known way to avoid crashing airplanes is to never fly them. And the only known way to raise a perfect and totally successful kid is to never have one. What fun is that? Read on and discover how this fighter pilot parent chases perfection, manages risk, and unconditionally loves his kids.

---

1 I can't share this story without also mentioning that Bug was killed in 1991 when his A-4E Skyhawk's only engine failed, followed by the failure of his ejection seat. He ran out of options.

FIRST-TIME SUCCESS IN THE MILITARY AND IN PARENTING

———

S uccess means different things to different people. For strike fighter squadron commanders, success usually means returning home with the same number of aircraft and people that you started with, and decisively executing every mission you are assigned. At the Navy fighter pilot level, it usually means performing your mission, supporting your wingmen, and landing aboard the ship the first time, every time. The emphasis here on first-time success penetrates every area of fighter pilot development, which is understandable given the costs associated with aircraft, weapon systems, collateral damage, and aircrew training. In warfare, it has gotten to the point where failure is no longer an option, and US air forces have set a pretty high standard.

What Does First-Time Success Look Like?

What are the secrets of first-time success in combat—or in parenting? How can children benefit from the fighter pilot experience? First, let me give you an illustration of what it looks like in the military.

In Operation Desert Storm, in just over a month's time in 1991, nearly 110,000 sorties were flown against a fairly advanced Iraqi threat. The US only lost twenty-seven aircraft and five helicopters during the entire conflict.

Then, in the first response to the 9/11 terrorist attacks, the major air operations in support of Operation Enduring Freedom lasting about two months concluded with 6,500 sorties flown against a much less sophisticated threat. There were no losses at all.

And finally, the Operation Iraqi Freedom Air Campaign, which lasted less than two months in 2003, ended with 41,404 sorties flown, and only seven aircraft lost to enemy fire. Losing one airplane or pilot is clearly a tragedy, but when you compare modern losses to past military operations, the results are astonishing. For perspective and context, the US lost on average 170 aircraft per day in World War II. We have come a long way in the pursuit of first-time success—albeit still not quite perfection.

The list of factors contributing to first-time success is endless: preparation, planning, practice, proficiency, knowledge, intelligence, optimal systems and tools, flexibility, adaptability, mental toughness, physical toughness, collaboration, coordination, composure, discipline—and the list goes on. It is my opinion that there is only one way to develop and hone each of those factors simultaneously, and that is through a process I call controlled failure.

Controlled Failure

Optimal performance and first-time success occur when a person is safely allowed to make mistakes—individually and as part of a team—in progressively more challenging scenarios. Failure is your friend. With my son, the youngest of four and the only boy, we noticed that he ran in an unusual way when playing youth micro soccer when he was five or six years old—to the point of concern. After watching a few of his games and seeing no improvement, I observed him during his other activities. The problem soon became obvious. As the "baby," and the substantially younger brother to three big sisters, he constantly was being picked up and carried everywhere. He wasn't allowed to make mistakes or perfect his running mechanics. We weren't doing him any favors. So we quickly returned to the controlled failure concept that my daughters had benefited from when they were little.

All the factors that go into first-time success must gradually be tested in order to evolve to a point of mastery. And then, and most important, any mistakes have to be honestly appraised and corrected, no matter how slight, before moving on to the next challenge. Ultimately in combat, you want quick, decisive, and overwhelming first-time success in many different areas simultaneously. This process of controlled failure has proven itself time and again, and it's the primary reason there is no greater fighting force in military history than the US military.

Crawl, Walk, Run

In the Navy, we call it "crawl, walk, run"—just like raising kids, right? We start from nothing, build and master basic skills, and then integrate those skills into more sophisticated and risky scenarios until we are ready for deployment and combat. If you've ever taught a teenager how to drive, you understand exactly how this might work (especially if you live in Southern California, where every drive seems like combat). And then, when proficiency and currency start to fade, you go through the whole process again—for instance, when your teenager comes home from college and hasn't been behind the wheel for some time.

If this type of preparation is done right, there are no big surprises on game day. For me, aside from real bullets and missiles coming at you, controlled failure made combat actually seem easier than training. By the time you get there, the confidence you feel and the trust you have that everything will function properly and everyone will do their job is extremely high, but not too high. On game day, everything has been perfected and integrated in training, and coordinated in execution. By doing all these things first, only then can you adequately plan, make good decisions, and improve your chance of high first-time success. This is much easier to say than to do, mainly because it requires patience and discipline.

"Controlled failure is the price that parents must be willing to pay to help their children achieve their dreams."

Controlled failure is exactly how Navy fighter pilots and other military professionals make the complex and dangerous look routine. It is the defining process for mastering and sustaining a complex set of skills while building earned confidence and a positive winning attitude. There are no shortcuts or substitutions. Controlled failure is the price that parents must be willing to pay to help their children achieve their dreams.

It probably goes without saying, but safety is an extremely important piece of this process. When you plan to fail, you also must plan to control the consequences of failure. You need a safety net. Controlled failure and risk management go hand in hand. As speed, pace, and complexity advance (and as your child grows older), the safety net must also expand to address the new safety environment, but in such a way that it doesn't compromise the payoff: advancement to the next level.

The Navy calls this operational risk management (ORM).

Operational Risk Management (ORM)

The concept of ORM is pretty simple and can be applied to anything. For Navy fighter pilots, safety nets are typically represented as a set of hard-and-fast rules that are nonnegotiable. This is especially evident in the areas of carrier operations and advanced tactical training.

For example, in order to maintain night carrier landing currency, you would have to perform a night carrier landing every seven days. If you miss that window, then you have to perform remedial tasks, in terms of extra day flights and landings, to regain currency. It is aggravating at times, but it's necessary in a controlled failure environment.

For kids, I'd liken it to taking a final exam. As the semester progresses, students often become less proficient in the earlier lessons and have to go back and "re-familiarize" themselves with the material before the big test.

It's also worth mentioning that controlled failure hard-and-fast rules can always be waived by someone, although this typically doesn't happen. On the ship, the aircraft carrier captain can change the night landing rule, but I've never seen it done. Why? Because data shows that the risk of a landing related mishap jumps significantly after seven days. At that point, the safety net becomes too small. This is where discipline and patience must prevail.

Our parenting hard-and-fast rules for final exams include limitations on entertainment, getting good rest, and quizzing knowledge areas that have been dormant. In our house, my wife has waiver authority, and she too rarely uses it.

In the air-to-air training arena, there are multiple risks that could easily push even a controlled failure event toward an unsafe and non-productive state. The hard-and-fast rules here include currency requirements, minimum altitude limits, airspeed limits, weather minimums,

continued

and so on. We even have to warm up before we start controlled failure training. Our version of a warm-up allows us to prepare our body for high g-forces and also make sure the jet is ready for controlled failure.

In this arena, the biggest risk—and therefore the most important rule—is in the area of ground avoidance. We set a minimum altitude of 5,000 feet above the ground (referred to as the hard deck). When anyone penetrates it, we immediately stop training. It's such a big deal that it even had its own scene in a major motion picture. Tom Cruise's character, Pete "Maverick" Mitchell, in the movie *Top Gun*, was severely admonished for flying below the hard deck, despite his excuse that "it was only for a few seconds."

This controlled failure risk management process is contagious. In my time, almost all fighter pilots developed and applied the "live to fight another day" standard to almost everything they did. If controlled failure risk couldn't be avoided or sufficiently reduced, training was either terminated or suspended. Again, discipline and patience must prevail. Once you figure out that your safety net no longer fits, you need to stop what you're doing or get a new one.

The process of tailoring the right size safety net is where the hard work is done. It can't be too restrictive, or controlled failure becomes no failure, and therefore no growth or learning will occur. And it can't be too skimpy, or controlled failure becomes a catastrophic failure. The fighter pilot safety net is very dynamic. It is constantly being calibrated for the environment, the individual, the team, and risk tolerance. In other words, you have to know what types of controlled failures are acceptable and what types are not.

It took many years to develop the basic safety net for naval aviation's controlled failure process, but the constant tinkering and improvement established the US as the most dominant air power in the world. In the

Navy, it also reduced the accident rate from 776 aircraft lost in 1956 to only 3 lost in 2003. That is a 26,000 percent improvement.

With the basic safety net covered, most of the fine tuning happens during preflight planning, prelaunch huddles, and especially during flight when conditions change. A "live to fight another day" mindset is so ingrained in the way fighter pilots do business, that it purrs along continually and effortlessly in the background. And although the risk tolerance limits can be really pressed using this process, there is never a situation where death or the loss of an aircraft is acceptable or becomes more valuable than the alternative. Despite all the efforts that go into the controlled failure process, it is important to remember that risk can never be completely eliminated. Sometimes you just can't catch or anticipate everything.

Dealing with the Unpredictable and the Unrecoverable

On what was supposed to be my last night as the air wing LSO (remember legendary LSO Bug Roach telling me about situations beyond anyone's control?), a serious risk-management scenario presented itself. As we were rounding the southern tip of India, en route to the north Arabian Sea and a waning Operation Desert Storm, we were committed to refreshing our night currency so we would be completely ready when we arrived. During transit, night flying was severely limited due to the challenge of maneuvering the ship for flight operations while also staying on our intended transit track, so we took the opportunity to fly at night whenever we could. That particular night was the first opportunity in a long time to do so.

We had a full night schedule—four events with ten to fourteen aircraft in each. We also had some pretty serious challenges. There was a high cloud layer that dimmed the stars, and the moon was useless to us on the other side of the planet so visibility was compromised. Other than being in a mine with the lights out, there is no other darkness quite like it. Plus, as is typical in this area of the world, the Indian Ocean sea swells were pushing our gigantic ship around. We also had no place to divert aircraft should the ship or an aircraft experience a significant problem. This was not an uncommon scenario, but we needed to engage in some additional and aggressive risk management. Our safety net was really tiny and needed some alterations.

Despite the challenging conditions, we decided to fly. However, we limited the controlled failure opportunity to "A" Team pilots—pilots with proven exceptional landing performance. I personally went to each squadron ready room and reviewed their schedule. Most squadrons had already self-regulated (made their own risk adjustments), but one thing caught my eye. I recognized a pilot who had a long history of marginal performance. He was under constant scrutiny and had many dangerous landings to his name, despite being a fairly experienced aviator. To expand the safety net, I asked the squadron to remove him from their schedule. They obliged, or so I thought.

As the first group of aircraft prepared for their night landing miles away, I decided to go up to the LSO platform (this is where LSOs control airplanes adjacent to the landing area) to observe. As the primary and backup LSOs took their positions, I wedged myself out of the way in the rear near the net (a place where LSOs can jump to safety in case of a crash), unbeknownst to everyone else. Thankfully, I had never had to use the net for my own personal safety.

As the LSOs completed their radio and equipment checks, the lights from the first of fourteen aircraft appeared on the horizon. I scanned the screen for the pilot names, and my stomach sank. The one and only pilot I had excused from flying happened to be in the first aircraft coming down. Not good, but at least for the moment, the deck was cooperating and fairly stable. It wouldn't last.

At a half mile out, it looked like he was positioned to make a good landing. However, the randomness of the sea swells worked against him. About ten seconds from landing, the back end of the ship suddenly elevated dramatically. The pilot was advised of the situation and cautioned to hold his rate of descent, which he did inititally. Unfortunately, though, he elevated slightly. The LSOs alerted him so he could correct his overpowered position.

With about five seconds remaining to touchdown, the deck movement peaked and started to cycle back down. What the pilot did next was unpredictable and instantaneously unrecoverable. Anticipating going high, he pulled his throttles to idle and pushed his nose down. When I heard his engines spool down, I knew it was over for him—and maybe even for all of us on the LSO platform. I immediately jumped into the net, descending via its steel frame, into a space directly below the LSO platform, hoping that I had just made a big fool of myself.

But I hadn't. As I lay on my back in the net, I heard a noise that sounded like a dumpster being dropped off a ten-story building. I opened my eyes to see the horizon change from pitch-black to bright orange. Other LSOs started joining me in the net. To avoid being at the bottom of the LSO dog pile, I made my way back up to the flight deck just in time to see the pilot's F-14 Tomcat cockpit slide off the landing area backward and fall toward the dark Indian Ocean.

Seconds later, the F-14's crew initiated ejection. One seat went out over the water. The other went back over the ship. The crewmember who landed in the water survived and was rescued by helicopter. The other—the pilot—crashed on the flight deck before his parachute had fully deployed, and he died on impact. The flight deck was a mess. Grieving and lessons learned would have to wait.

There were pieces of the wrecked jet covering the entire landing area. Some were large, but most were very small. Multiple fires littered the broken aircraft's track as well as the area below the ramp, called the fantail. Our first priority was to get them extinguished. The firefighting foam system was activated, leaving the deck and wreckage covered with a coating of thick, white foam. But more importantly, there were thirteen more aircraft waiting to land. Some were very low on fuel, and our ship was their only option.

Despite the tragedy created through a risk-management oversight, redemption was eventually found in the controlled failure process that we had endured over time. It worked like this: The teams on the flight deck quickly removed the debris, cleared the landing area, and launched an aircraft capable of refueling those in the air waiting to land—all within twenty minutes or so. The remaining aircraft, with air controller-assisted sequencing, prepared for landing as the ship drivers on the bridge maneuvered the ship for optimal recovery wind and a more stable flight. My LSO partner and I manned the LSO platform, and we began bringing them aboard.

The pilots flew exceptional landings despite being under intense pressure. Perfection was the only option by then. We closed the night with everyone back on board. It was a total team effort that was completely brokered through our preparation for first-time success. From ever-escalating complexity and challenge in drills and training scenarios to being disciplined about risk management and risk controls, our success that night can only be attributed to controlled failure.

Parenting and Controlled Failure

As a parent, you probably want your children to be successful at many things. If you were to create a list of what those things were and how you can help them along that journey, your list might look something like this:

☆ What process will I use to determine their natural passions and to develop a crawl, walk, run approach (controlled failure)?

☆ How will I help them achieve their dreams in terms of ever-escalating challenge, complexity, and discipline?

☆ What safety nets will I use to accelerate mastery without crushing their enthusiasm and passion for the things they love?

It is my opinion that there is a growing tendency, whether purposeful or not, for parents to cheat the process by never letting their children fail at anything. Medals and awards for showing up and participating seem to be just fine to some. Out of love or convenience, some parents never let their children approach the scary edge of the envelope where real growth and learning happen. If you're not failing, you're not trying, so to speak.

"Failure is not a bad thing. Failure is your friend."

Failure is not a bad thing. Failure is your friend. Fail frequently, but fail forward or fail differently in order to learn and improve. Failure breeds experience. Experience breeds wisdom. Wisdom breeds future success and good decision-making. Trading all these wonderful benefits for a false sense of self-esteem and a short-lived confidence is not a very good bargain in the long term.

At the other extreme, there are some parents who demand that their kids be successful at everything. That is a tall order. It is tough enough to master two or three things you are passionate about, let alone mastering many additional things you are not. Precious few can pull that off. The pressure is intense. The fun factor is low. Ultimately, instead of mastering your passions, you become a jack of all trades, master of none.

Each child is different. They have their own individual performance envelope, like a high-performance jet, and parents can add tremendous value by knowing where that edge is and allowing their children to explore it using controlled failure methods. Sometimes the edge is physical, sometimes it is knowledge, and sometimes it is just plain apprehension and fear. Avoiding failure at all costs is not in anyone's best interest. It only introduces other risks that tend to be more insidious and more devastating later in life. You won't be able to protect your kids forever.

As I mentioned earlier, certain risks are never acceptable. Child predators of all kinds lurk everywhere. Catastrophic injury is clearly unacceptable for your child as well. As a fighter pilot, analogies to these unacceptable risks include successful enemy action, mishaps, and aircraft losses. Where child safety is concerned, there can be no compromises, yet if controlled failure is applied and you are disciplined about risk management, you will have already acknowledged the risk potential and will have invested in the appropriate controls that will allow you to persevere and increase your child's likelihood for first-time success at the most challenging levels. Just as in combat, you respect the threat, avoid the threat where possible, build or use threat sanctuaries, and monitor the threat for any changes. Ultimately, controlled failure leads to better decision-making and the ability to define—and therefore measure—success.

Measuring Success

During Operation Iraqi Freedom, one measure of success for aircraft carriers was the ability to provide over 150 strike sorties (launch and recovery) per day over three continuous days. This uncommon level of effort placed an incredible strain on aircrew, maintenance personnel, flight deck personnel, logistic systems, and airspace control. It was extremely painful and dangerous, but it was a must-not-fail expectation. We needed to be able to do this in order to be successful elsewhere. Therefore, in order not to fail in combat, we had to preemptively control failure in training. By incrementally building that stress level, we found and fixed significant gaps, we became a better team, and we significantly improved our probability of combat success. Controlled failure is a process of recalibration and continuous improvement. Sometimes you just can't possibly know or predict vulnerabilities until they are tested under stressful and realistic conditions. You see this with sports teams when they play against two opponents of different levels. The things that work against a lesser opponent end up revealing a vulnerability in competition against a stronger opponent.

Success, Hard Work, and Passion

Real success is not automatic or guaranteed—not in flight training and not in parenting. It is earned through the process of harvesting lessons along the way, closing gaps, and gaining valuable experience as you chase perfection.

How are air campaigns and parenting comparable? Actually, the process of defining success and controlling failure is identical. Just like fighter pilots before they go into air campaigns, before you send your kids out into the world you properly train, test, supervise, and monitor them. You wouldn't just drop them off at the mall or throw them in the pool and see what happens. As they grow older, and success plans evolve, keeping a close and watchful eye becomes more problematic, but if you've invested in a controlled failure process, and your kids have proven themselves ready, a high probability of success is waiting for them, and you.

If your children desire trying out successfully for a sports team, getting an A on a major exam, or passing their driving test on the first try, getting to those goals through the rigor in training and risk management that pilots use for first-time combat success is not a bad way to go. Over time, kids will understand the importance and value of preparing for first-time success. Understanding, appreciating, and enjoying are not the same thing unfortunately. Hard work is involved.

Let's face it, hard work is not fun. It's especially not fun if you don't have passion for the achievement that you seek. With fighter pilots, most are extremely passionate about flying. They love it and want to be the best at it. Still, while night flying and being away from your family may be essential elements of success, few would argue that either could be considered fun. Success ultimately depends on how you approach the not-so-fun stuff.

I have three daughters and a son who all love playing sports and are technically and athletically gifted. At one point in each of their athletic journeys, they had to face the fact that there were two other elements they needed—sports IQ and fitness. Understanding and applying sports tactics combined with physical endurance became key differentiators at the highest competitive levels. But investing in those attributes was nowhere near as fun as just playing the game. They had to study. They had to work out. It wasn't fun.

As each kid experienced diminishing success in the sport they loved, they eventually saw the value in committing effort and discipline toward the boring and painful.

I'm a firm believer that each kid has a natural, inherent set of talents or gifts. Sometimes, as parents, you may have to nudge your kids until they have the maturity and desire it takes to do things themselves. Some can sing, some are good at math, some are comedians, and some are born to be fighter pilots. Whatever it is, that is where you'll find their passion. By linking passion, gifts, and vision, they'll have the highest probability of first-time success because preparation won't seem like work (passion), and they already have a distinct advantage (gifts).

Unfortunately, many parents either misidentify their children's gifts or try to replace them with something that they'd prefer them to have. Some people just aren't meant to fly airplanes. Some people aren't meant to be professional football players. Fortunately, there is a fairly easy way to find out what your child's gifts are.

> "Sometimes, as parents, you may have to nudge your kids until they have the maturity and desire it takes to do things themselves."

Think about when they were eight or nine. At that age, there is usually something that they do so frequently that you constantly have to tell them to stop. At age eight, my son was on a kick where he had figured out every variation of the *The Legend of Zelda* video game theme song on the piano. He didn't play any other songs, but he would race to the piano when we got home so he could play it. Even worse, he dragged unwitting guests to the piano so he could play the song for them—again and again and again. I couldn't get it out of my head. I eventually realized that his true gift was not mastery of a theme song but mastery of the technical, joined with the cognitive needs of the game environment. His real passion probably was in the area of intellectual stimulation where time-sensitive problem-solving requires both physical as well as mental skills.

When you find those gifts, start shaping their trajectory toward higher order objectives. Help your children catch excellence. There is nothing more tragic than wasted talent. With passion-fueled gifts and a proving ground where kids can fail gracefully in a controlled environment, they will quickly build upon each experience and form a habit for first-time success in each new and more challenging endeavor. But be careful. The failures you control can't be too embarrassing, scary, or frustrating. That usually happens when you push and expect success too quickly.

In flight training, pilots don't move on until they've mastered lower-order skills. If they were allowed to skip ahead right to the graduation flight, they would ultimately fail miserably, and it would be very dangerous.

Pushing too hard and expecting quick success is exactly how we made my middle daughter hate water polo and ultimately swimming. She was a great swimmer, worked extremely hard, and was unbelievably coachable. Some would even say she had a gift for it. As she quickly outpaced her peer group in the water, it was clear that she was becoming bored, so we moved her up. Now this wasn't an ordinary club water polo program she was in—this was the Coronado Aquatics Club, renowned for placing several alumni on national and Olympic teams.

By moving up, our daughter was subjected to extremely challenging workouts and games against bigger, powerful, and more experienced girls—including her sister. For her, water polo went from being fun to being intimidating and scary. It soon became a matter of mere survival rather than learning and developing. We had lost control of her failure environment. Instead of gaining experience through controlled failures mixed with many small successes, we literally put her in way over her head. In doing so, we instantaneously created a dread of and even hatred for the sport.

It's also possible to create the same kind of aversion by seeing someone else fail spectacularly doing the same thing you are expected to do. In 1984, myself and a group of fighter pilots had just finished qualifying to fly the A-7E Corsair II aboard ship day and night when we watched a video of a horrific ramp strike. The pilot in the crash had been in our shoes a few months earlier but was now dead. His crash wasn't the classic dark night, bad weather scenario; it was daytime, and the weather was great. If the ship hadn't been moving so much, it would have been a perfect carrier aviation day.

But, just like the night crash I described earlier, the tiny landing area was subjected to twenty to thirty foot pitches. As is typical in these situations, at the critical moment when the deck cycled from extremely high to extremely low, the pilot responded with an aggressive correction, immediately placing himself in extreme danger as the deck came back up again.

He had no time to recover. The aircraft struck the back of the ship just under the cockpit and broke into two pieces. The cockpit slid forward into the water. The pilot never attempted ejection and was killed. It was pretty sobering to watch that video, wondering—with our limited experience—if we had what it took to prevent that from happening to us. At least one of us came to the conclusion that he didn't belong in our special club. He returned his wings and chose another profession. The rest of us consumed the lessons that had just been written in blood and moved forward.

As I coach younger kids in lacrosse, I often have to address this intimidation factor, as they are typically undersized relative to their older competitors. Despite their superior skills and tactics, they fixate on the size disparity, especially following a crushing hit. I've found that as long as I continue to remind them of their advantages and manage their success through tactics, substitutions, and matchups, it goes a long way toward pushing them through the fear barrier.

Confidence, Creativity, and Doing Things You're Not Prepared for

There are two more important benefits of chasing perfection and catching excellence: confidence and creativity. Sometimes urgency or a rapidly changing environment forces you to act before you are ready and do things you have not specifically prepared for. In aviation, in warfare, and in life, this seems to happen all too frequently. But if you have been chasing perfection and nearing excellence over time, you will eventually possess the mental tools to adapt, improvise, and use your vast array of finely tuned skills in unique and creative ways. Such was the case for my carrier strike group aboard the USS *Constellation* in the early days of Iraqi Freedom in 2003.

Shortly after US ground forces moved north toward Baghdad, the entire area was besieged by the storm of the century. Strong winds stirred up all the dust and sand in the region (that's a lot of dirt and sand), which quickly darkened the sky and reduced visibility to zero. All land air bases were shut down, along with two of three aircraft carriers in the north Arabian Sea. Only one aircraft carrier, the USS *Constellation*, still had weather minimums of a half-mile visibility and a two-hundred-foot cloud ceiling—but just barely.[2]

There couldn't have been a worse time for an immediate, urgent,

---

2   This was the same weather event that caused Private First Class Jessica Lynch's convoy to get lost and exposed to attack by Iraqi militia forces. She was injured when her vehicle crashed, and she was captured. She became the first Iraqi Freedom prisoner of war and was later rescued by elite special operators.

and high-priority demand for air support, but that was exactly what happened. Alarming and consistent intelligence reports indicated that a very large Iraqi military convoy was moving south from Baghdad using the storm as a sanctuary from air attack. Even more concerning was the possibility that the Iraqi convoy possessed chemical weapons. The US ground forces were sitting ducks. They couldn't move, they couldn't see, and they had no air cover. Plus, when the rains finally came, the sand and dust became windblown mud.

All participating coalition air forces were asked what they could do to help to counter the convoy. Only one, the air wing from the USS *Constellation*, had any real chance of rendering assistance. The aircraft carrier was in the only remaining area that could still launch and recover aircraft, but weather conditions were deteriorating. If they were going to respond, they would have to take on significant risk. They would be walking a slippery tightrope without any safety nets. In other words, it was very likely the pilots would have no place suitable to land when they returned. If they were forced to eject—assuming they didn't get dragged to death by their wind-propelled parachutes—no one would be available to pick them up, and their ability to target a convoy in such adverse weather was uncertain.

This looked like a one-way, terminal mission. Yet, as a result of first-time success preparation, earned confidence, and proven creativity, it was ultimately concluded that the crews that would participate had the skill sets, proficiency, and currency to be successful, and a decision to launch four F/A-18s was made. The twelve Joint Standoff Weapons (JSOW) from these four aircraft successfully dispersed the Iraqi convoy, and the eminent threat to vulnerable Marine ground forces was thankfully averted. Despite the odds against them, this crew successfully completed a mission they had never practiced, and they returned to land in the most challenging conditions. Whew! It was a close one, to say the least, but the process of chasing perfection and catching excellence through controlled failure created options that otherwise would not have existed.

When Is the Right Time to Go for It?

So how do you decide when it's the right time to have a go at something bigger? That's a tough call. Since it is impossible to guarantee perfection in anything, it comes down to perceived acceptable risk. That risk includes both the risk of failure in execution as well as the risk of not trying at all. Probability of success is zero if you don't try. Probability of success is something higher than zero if you at least make an attempt, but less than 100 percent. For kids, confidence is probably the hardest thing to muster. They are often very comfortable and secure where they are and therefore resistant to the next challenge. Yet parents know it is the next challenge that will propel them forward.

What I've learned, though, as both a fighter pilot and a parent, is that the controlled failure approach has no equal when it comes to creating the confidence and resiliency required to take on new challenges and new environments. I've really seen it with my kids and their social life. Having moved so much, my kids faced frequent school changes and new social situations. But as the beneficiaries of controlled failure parenting, each move was significantly less stressful, and they projected that growing social confidence into the other parts of their young lives.

Most parents, coaches, and teachers know when a child is ready for something bigger or more challenging—well ahead of the child. Confidence seems to always lag, no matter what the age. So parents really need to help drive their kids to the next level until they become comfortable with discomfort and can do it themselves. This also helps prepare them for adversity and the unpredictable.

In real life, challenges are often thrust upon us by circumstances beyond our control. There seems to be a lot of ready-or-not, here-we-go surprises. I must confess, I don't ever remember feeling completely ready for any challenging task or mission, but in retrospect, I found quiet strength and confidence in my controlled failure roots, especially when it came to managing uncertainty and chaos. A typical day for parents!

"For parenting, good habits and routines beat back uncertainty and surprises."

In the military, we have a saying that "an 80 percent plan executed now is better than a 100 percent plan executed late." How do you increase your odds when you're constantly battling imperfection, chaos, and uncertainty? When the show must go on, you can continue to improve your chances by grooming the most important tools, adding redundancies, and developing contingencies. For combat missions, it is considered extremely negligent not to do all three. The really high performing squadrons take this approach for everything, including friendly bombing competitions. For high-performance parenting in an unpredictable world, interleaving these fighter pilot success multipliers will have the same impact. Whether it's a student council election or a mock trial competition, good habits and routines are important when chasing perfection and catching excellence. For parenting, good habits and routines beat back uncertainty and surprises.

Bombing Competition

During our long transits to intended operating areas, night landing proficiency isn't the only skill that suffers. Air wings seldom get the opportunity to practice bombing. When they do get to bomb, the target is usually a smoke charge dropped in the water. On rare occasions, the aircraft carrier will tow a small barge behind it and allow aircraft to take turns either bombing or strafing the towed target. It never fails that when a target is towed, a squadron bombing competition is announced. Such was the case on one of my deployments in the early '90s. There are rules to these competitions.

Only one pilot from each squadron can participate. Each aircraft has to drop three consecutive bombs. Any failure to drop is considered a 300-foot miss. If any aircraft violates an altitude or heading safety rule, it will also be scored as either a 300-foot miss or a disqualification. The whole ship is watching. There is no practice and no do-overs. It's all about first-time success.

Despite our lack of bombing proficiency, we were committed to winning the competition. It was a matter of professional pride and squadron morale. In order to improve our chances, we added a few "uncertainty" management enhancements that no one else employed.

The five participating squadrons all had about the same pilot bombing proficiency and used similar computed weapons release systems in their airplanes. The bomb was a twenty-five-pound practice bomb that each pilot had dropped thousands of times in training. The target was a 15-foot by 30-foot inflatable barge that was towed about 500 feet behind the carrier. The time of flight of the bomb, when released in a twenty-degree dive, was about four seconds. What we didn't know was the ship's speed or the winds, crucial pieces of data.

We decided to use the most proficient pilot in our squadron for the competition. We selected the airplane that had the best bombing history and spent some time grooming the systems that improved accuracy (radar and inertial navigation). We had a spare aircraft ready to go as well. After launch, the pilot performed the delivery maneuvers several times in order to perfect the delivery profile and aim-point placement. The other squadrons did the same things. Our most significant advantage was how we planned for wind and ship speed.

Knowing how much wind and speed could affect the bomb after release, we prepared a plan to determine both, communicate that to the pilot, and make the appropriate adjustments to where the pilot aimed. After creating a simple matrix with wind, speed, and aim-point offsets, a second pilot sat in an aircraft and set up his system to have instantaneous speed readouts and talk to the delivery pilot on a secure radio. With a very precise offset aiming cue, accuracy could be significantly enhanced.

Everything went as planned. The pilot launched and practiced his profile using the data the second pilot was providing. The second pilot also went through a checklist that included all the switch positions for bombing and recording the runs. During post-competition analysis, pilot tapes would be reviewed for safety violations. No recording was the same as a no drop.

Approaching our first "hot" run, everything was set. Switches were verified, an offset aim-point was predicted (one-and-a-half barge lengths ahead of the barge), and tapes were on. As the aircraft pulled off, we could see the small blue bomb in flight. It literally hit the attachment point between the tow cable and the barge—a direct hit. The other pilots came close, but not that close. We made a slight adjustment, and the next bomb hit the target in the first third of the barge—another direct hit. The other pilots improved a little but still didn't come as close as us.

The final run was no different. No adjustment was necessary. We could see the final bomb come off. As long as it came close and there

continued

were no safety violations, we would win easily. By this stage, not surprisingly, the final bomb hit nearly in the same place as the second
bomb—another direct hit. The VFA-27 Chargers became the air wing
bombing champs—at least until the next competition.

First-Time Success Is Never Accidental

First-time success is never accidental. It channels the lessons learned
from every training failure and training success. It acknowledges realistic gaps and attempts to close them as tightly as possible with sound
risk management adjustments. It has backup options should conditions
change dramatically. And it places high value on all contributing elements, including the not-so-fun stuff.

Don't shortchange your kids as they chase perfection. The challenges
they face shouldn't be either too easy or too hard. Each gate they pass
through should include recoverable failures that earn experience, not
aversion. Teach them to embrace failures and challenges because that is
where growth and learning occurs. Failure should be a badge of honor.
It implies experience, growth, maturity, and a step closer toward perfection. Remind them that they'll always be forced or asked to perform
before they think they're ready. If they have evolved using a controlled
failure process, they will be able to rely on and trust their journey and
the results it will produce. They will be the "best trained, most feared."

★★★

FIGHTER PILOT PARENT TAKEAWAYS— First-Time Success

1. Find your child's passion and invest in it.

2. Whatever you are telling your children to stop doing when they are nine years old (because they are doing it incessantly) is exactly where their passion lies.

3. Controlled failure encourages high first-time success.

4. First-time success is never accidental.

5. If you are not failing, you are not trying.

6. Failure is your friend.

7. Controlled failures shouldn't be too embarrassing, scary, or frustrating.

8. Controlled failure demands the right size safety net.

9. No one ever thinks they are ready, even when they actually are.

10. There is no such thing as risk-free parenting.

CHAPTER TWO

WHY THERE ARE NO ATHEISTS IN THE COCKPIT

———

Many years ago, I had the opportunity to be the keynote speaker at a Native American appreciation event. As a lacrosse player from New York, I had always been fascinated with Native American culture and the history of their uniquely original game. One of the guest speakers was a local shaman (medicine man). During his presentation, he introduced me to the medicine wheel concept. As I understand it, the medicine wheel represents the circle of life and focuses on internal balance and how everything is interconnected. When any of the four medicine wheel quadrants is out of balance, it creates distress or illness—which can't be remedied until balance is restored.

An Essential Balance

Although there are many different explanations for each quadrant, generally speaking they can be categorized as physical, emotional/social, wisdom/intellectual, and spiritual. As both a Christian and a fighter pilot, the medicine wheel concept—especially the spiritual part—really resonated with me.

I've always felt humans are wired with a need to worship something. And whatever it is, over time, they fully submit to it. If not God, then something else takes over—usually something unhealthy and destructive. We all know people who worship money, sex, popularity, celebrity, or even extreme adventure. Are they satisfied? Are they happy? I don't know anyone like that who would honestly admit to being happy or satisfied. Why not?

By using the medicine wheel, the reason becomes clear: Their spiritual quadrant is out of balance. There is a big, gaping hole where God and faith needs to be. Filling it with anything else creates chaos, dissonance, and potentially dangerous alternative pursuits.

Fighter pilots have a tendency to go all in for speed, g-force, and low altitude. Then, at some point in their career, they come to realize that their survival is more often a direct result of the grace and generosity of a divine force rather than the product of their own skill and decision-making. Up until that point in time, their death-defying activities have a tendency to subordinate God to a minor role in their circle of life. Even when a good friend dies in a crash, they often attribute it to the dead pilot's deficiencies and quickly convince themselves that they are better than that "lesser" colleague. Some take it to an extreme.

The pilots who scared me most were the ones that had no fear of death. When pressed, they typically had no recollection of ever being scared in a jet and usually enjoyed a reputation of rule-breaking and close calls on every training event or combat mission. The Navy calls these pilots "failing aviators." They typically ignore strict safety rules and are known to live dangerously. Failing aviators tend to subconsciously elevate themselves to God status and in doing so, seriously distort their medicine wheel. Tragically, it's the laws of nature, or God's rules, that usually catch up to them. Aside from those few pilots, you won't find an atheist in most cockpits.

Admittedly, like most young pilots, at one point I started to fall into the same trap. As I successfully graduated from each phase of flight training, my confidence grew, and with each new progression, God got less credit. Eventually, I was assigned to fly the A-7E Corsair II, an aircraft that most experts at the time considered the most challenging and most dangerous to operate. Some even called it a death machine. It was a single-engine, single-seat jet that relied on extremely low altitude for sanctuary as well as for surprise and attack. Living at 200 feet above the ground, we were extremely comfortable there.

When God Loses Credit

I was also landing on aircraft carriers in all kinds of weather, day and night, and I was getting pretty good at it. God was losing more and more credit as my successes piled up. Peer pressure didn't help either. I was trying to keep up with other pilots in terms of flight time, carrier landings, bombs dropped, and low-altitude prowess. As that part of my medicine wheel dominated, the other parts of my life faltered as I became compelled to fly as much as I could in order to get better and keep up.

The old adage that you can only tie the record for flying low had no real significance for me by then. In fact, after hearing about someone who had placed his extended tailhook in the water while flying at 400 knots over the ocean, a small group of us were convinced that we needed to be part of that elite club too. So off we went one day. Our plan was to stabilize at twenty-five feet while the others observed. At twenty-five feet we would gradually lower the airplane until the observer saw spray, and then we would pull up and switch.

My wingman, the pilot in the aircraft next to me, went first. He was cleared to descend, and it didn't take long until I saw a jet of seawater, what we call a rooster tail, develop under his jet, and I told him to pull up. Then it was my turn. My knuckles were white as I tried to descend in micrometers, fighting through the bumpy air near the ocean's surface. I vaguely recall holding my breath during the entire drop. Then, just as I was about to give up, I got the signal, and we climbed to safety (one hundred feet). Talk about stupid—yet we were elated and very proud of our new elite status. We could never share that story with anyone, though. You could lose your wings over stuff like that.

Then it happened. I was scheduled for one of the best flights a pilot could ever get. I was supposed to take a wingman on a low-altitude, high-speed approach to a target in the San Clemente Island target complex, and then pop up and deliver four 500-pound bombs. The bombing party consisted of four different groups of two aircraft, including ours, and we would be separated on the target by five minutes—plenty of time. For safety reasons, we would transmit each phase of our attack: inbound to the target, popping up to establish the delivery profile, rolling in on the target, pulling off the target, egressing away from the target, and clearing the target area. That way everyone would know what the group ahead was doing and could therefore make timing safety corrections if necessary. We were the last group and the last to drop our bombs.

Everything was going great. Based on the radio transmissions, everyone was hitting their target times, and we could start our run as planned. As we pushed, the flight ahead of us, two A-6 Intruders, had just begun their run. At our ten-mile checkpoint, the A-6s reported off and clear. What we didn't know at the time was that one of the two A-6s had separated from his lead and was lagging behind several miles. For some reason, he didn't seem to think it was important to share that information with us or his lead, and he failed to update us on the radio.

As we turned on all our weapon switches and prepared for an attack, we wrongly assumed the target was clear. At three miles from the target, I started my pull from 200 feet above the water. As I elevated, I remember thinking it was odd that there was smoke from only one set of bombs in the target area. I even snickered thinking that one of the A-6s ahead of us had screwed something up. Boy, was I in for a surprise!

At 475 knots and with the target in sight, I completed my climb profile to 5,000 feet and forty-five degrees nose high. As I hit my pull-down altitude, I reversed and pulled hard back to the target to set up at a twenty-degree dive for weapon delivery. Just as I hit my parameters to roll-wings level, I saw a blur—no, make that two blurs. As I was grasping for clarity, the picture emerged.

Above me and to my right was an A-6 Intruder in very close proximity—one hundred feet. As time slowed down, I realized that the last of his four 500-pound bombs was just leaving his aircraft. I had nowhere to go. If I pulled up or left, I'd hit his aircraft. If I turned right, I'd fly into a group of armed and ready-to-detonate bombs. I decided to simply "get skinny" and fly between them both. Anticipating a collision, I braced for impact and felt around for my ejection-seat handle. Aside from a lot of noise and a little vibration, nothing happened. I slipped through, and I survived.

I thanked God—many times. After we got back to the ship, I was furious with the pilot who had nearly killed me. We figured that I came within millimeters of either flying into a bomb or into an airplane. The consequence would have been the same: certain death. My skill and training hadn't saved me. My quick thinking and decisiveness hadn't saved me. It was either dumb luck or divine providence. I gave credit to God.

An old naval aviation joke worth sharing starts with a pilot who was having significant problems getting aboard his ship. It was the worst kind of nighttime: no visible moon or stars, making the sky completely black. The deck was moving, his heads-up display (HUD) had malfunctioned, and he was having engine trouble. Every time he tried to land, he either got waved off or his hook missed all the wires— either because he was too high, the hook bounced over them, or the hook swung too far left or right. After his fifth attempt, he was getting low on fuel and decided he needed help. He asked God to make all his problems go away and get him aboard on the next pass.

"It seems that for most pilots and parents, that moment of surrender occurs when they're out of ideas, they're helpless, or when bad things happen."

Suddenly, like magic, the airplane started flying itself. It followed every input the final controller gave him, and he was set up perfectly for the approach. Despite adverse winds and dramatic deck movement, the jet managed to fly perfect glideslope and lineup. The pilot was amazed and extremely thankful as the jet continued to fly a perfect landing profile without his direct involvement. As the jet rolled out into the landing area, the pilot said to God, "I've got it now—everyone knows you don't taxi very well."

A Pilot's (and a Parent's) Relationship with God

That old aviation joke highlights the fundamental relationship we have with God. There is a God who loves you infinitely, serves you, and is always there for you. By surrendering to God, we in fact are worshiping Him. And you know you have surrendered when you trust God to work things out. The Bible says God will provide for all your needs—He only requires that you ask for His help, be content with what you have, give in faith, be honest, and trust Him.

It seems that for most pilots and parents, that moment of surrender occurs when they're out of ideas, they're helpless, or when bad things happen. For parents it starts way before birth. We were constantly worried and felt helpless when notoriously ambiguous prenatal tests came back either inconclusive or showed an abnormality requiring additional tests. We quickly surrendered.

After my little incident, I started flying with God all the time. I even let Him taxi a few times. I was committed to meeting Him halfway when asking for help. I wasn't afraid, too proud, or embarrassed. It became natural and comforting knowing I had that kind of support 24/7. My medicine wheel started to get back in balance again.

When Simple Gets Hard

Not long after my near-death experience over San Clemente Island, I encountered a longer duration scare. As we started our deployment and were halfway between California and Hawaii, we were tasked with demonstrating our ability to execute a 2,000-mile night strike. We decided that eight A-6s would be the bomb droppers. The plan called for the A-6s to launch late at night and be immediately refueled from A-7s configured as tankers. From there they would rendezvous with big Air Force tankers and refuel multiple times, drop their bombs, refuel again with the Air Force, and then come back to land. They would be airborne for at least eight hours. I was scheduled as one of the night A-7 tankers.

My job was to launch first, scout out a good area for rendezvous, and when I had my three A-6s with me, start steering toward Hawaii while giving them 3,500 pounds of gas apiece. (In aviation, we describe fuel amounts in pounds versus gallons.) The mission was pretty simple—plus there was a big moon out.

After I launched, simple got hard. A weather system had joined us. There was only one clear area for rendezvous, and it was nearly thirty miles from where we were supposed to be. Two of my A-6s were not monitoring the briefed radio frequency, so they were late getting the update and late joining. That little delay put me right on the edge of having enough gas to give them their share and still make it back to the ship. As soon as we started heading west toward Hawaii, we entered thick clouds. The A-6s stayed extremely close in order to keep sight. We also had other flights above and below us just a few hundred feet, but we couldn't see them. And two of my A-6s were still not monitoring the radio frequency.

My aircraft had a special contraption mounted under the left wing that contained a rubber hose with a basket at the end that, when extended, allows Navy jets to connect (via a refueling probe on the receiving aircraft's nose) to transfer fuel between the two planes. I gave the light signals indicating I was about to put out my hose and basket. I wasn't really supposed to extend my hose until the area directly behind me was clear, but I still had an A-6 cuddling with me who wasn't tuned to my radio frequency, so I decided to put it out a little and pull it back in. It worked. The A-6s got in line off to my left side, and we started off-loading fuel. The first guy took forever getting into the basket. More delays. Then, after I gave him his 3,500 pounds of gas, I couldn't get him to back out and move aside. After I flashed my lights several times, he got the idea and cleared for the next plane.

Thankfully, number two was much quicker and went through the process without incident. He must have been the only one on the right radio frequency.

The last plane was extremely slow getting in the basket. Admittedly, it's not fun flying formation in the clouds, let alone getting gas. It took him multiple attempts. After I gave him every last drop I could spare and then some, he didn't budge. He stayed in the basket as I continued to get dangerously low on fuel. At the point where I was out of options, I pulled my hose in and watched him flail a little in my mirrors. But he still wouldn't budge. I had an A-6 to my left, right, and behind, with flights above me and below me. Plus, I was now in an emergency fuel situation.

I did what anyone would do, I guess. I pulled up abruptly so all the aircraft wouldn't be able to stay with me, and then turned hard to avoid the aircraft above. It worked. I was finally free of those pesky parasites. The relief was only temporary.

As soon as I turned around, everything in the cockpit went dark. I reached for the generator switch and cycled it off and then back on. I was worried that I'd quickly get disoriented flying in the clouds with no reference to my nose and wing positions.

I was slightly relieved when the lights came back on, but without power for that brief moment, all my navigation systems were compromised and couldn't be trusted. I was now at the mercy of my standby gyroscope for my nose and wing positions and my standby compass (the kind of compass you can buy to put in your car) for heading. I only had an hour of fuel remaining, so I couldn't afford any delays in my return.

Without any navigation aids, I turned to a heading opposite from the one I had been on and started timing for forty minutes, the time duration I spent outbound. I was still in the clouds, but fuel was so critical that I maintained my altitude to get the most out of what I had left. Then I tried the radios. Nothing. Every frequency had static. I tried my radar, hoping to find the big fat aircraft carrier as quickly as possible. Nothing.

At night in the clouds, with forty minutes of fuel left, no radio contact, no navigation systems, and no radar contact, I asked God for help. I was out of ideas but not faith. I pressed on, and as my forty minutes elapsed, I started a slow descending turn hoping to break out of the clouds, get my eyes back, and expand my radar search.

Passing through 16,000 feet, I popped out of the clouds and was surprised to discover that the moon was now visible and the weather was exceptionally clear below—but still no ship. I tried my radios again. As I went through another round of frequencies, I heard something. It was the approach frequency.

I waited patiently for what seemed like a minute, and then I heard it: "Hobo 411, turn left to final heading, three five zero." After Hobo 411 responded, I transmitted my call sign and emergency fuel situation hoping to be heard. After patiently waiting again, I got a response: "Hobo 405, say position." I explained my situation, and after doing a couple of turns to correlate my location with their radar, they found me and gave me a vector for approach. I was only fifteen miles away. I was now down to my last twenty minutes of fuel—plenty, I thought.

Then things got interesting—again. As I switched to the final control frequency, I heard the LSOs talking to another aircraft. "Roger Ball Corsair, decks down, you're on glideslope . . . you're a little high, right for lineup . . . deck's up you're high . . . power! Deck's down . . . deck's coming up—POWER! POWER! Wave off."

I thought to myself, *Great, now I have to land with my backup instruments and a pitching deck.* As I pressed in, I heard another aircraft attempt to land with the same degree of success. I was next.

A Solid Partnership with God

I recalled the hundreds of times I had practiced this exact scenario in simulators, and I remembered who my copilot was, and my confidence soared. With about ten minutes of fuel left, the critical moment arrived. "405 Corsair Ball, 1.8, no HUD, no instruments." The LSOs responded, "Roger Ball, you're on glideslope . . . a little right for lineup . . . you're on glideslope . . . you're a little low, a little power . . . easy with it . . . power . . . nice job, 405."

I made it. God didn't fly the aircraft for me, but He gave me the composure and discipline I needed. He also reminded me how aggressively I had been chasing perfection, which gave me confidence. I thanked Him and taxied, mostly on my own, forward for shut down. As I was getting chained down, my flight deck chief climbed up the side of the aircraft and wanted to talk. I opened the canopy, and he yelled above all the noise, "We need you to fly again if you're good with it." Normally I would have jumped at the chance, but something was clearly wrong with the jet, and I was mentally exhausted. I declined. That was a good decision.

Even the Most Gifted Fail

As I gained more experience and then transitioned to F/A-18 Hornets, I began to realize that even some of the most gifted and talented pilots died in crashes. Not only were they great aviators, but some were also extraordinary people and faithful Christians. Flying with God helped, but it clearly didn't cover everything. It was easy to explain when a pilot did something really stupid or when a pilot was godless. They weren't worthy of grace, right? But it was a whole other animal when the person was the salt of the earth and someone you respected. How could bad things happen to gifted, smart, pious, and genuinely good people? And if it happened to them, what protections did I have?

When I was a squadron maintenance officer, I was blessed with one of the most talented engine technicians in the Navy. He worked tirelessly, he was highly competent, he was a teacher and leader, and he had an amazing personality. He loved and worshiped God, and he inspired everyone around him to be better, including me. We also had something very special in common—our wives were pregnant and shared the same due date.

We were on deployment throughout the pregnancies, but we shared daily updates and joked about our role as fathers. As it turns out, we would return home just a week before the end of our wives' terms. My wife gave birth to a beautiful and healthy daughter. It was a wonderful time. As we celebrated my return from deployment simultaneously with the birth of our second child, I wondered how my squadron pregnancy partner was doing.

When I checked in with his supervisor, the news was not good. His wife had delivered a boy, but he was far from healthy. Many of his tiny organs were dysfunctional, and it was just a matter of time before he would die. When he eventually passed, I was floored. I even felt guilty for receiving such tremendous blessings myself. It wasn't fair. My squadron partner and his wife didn't deserve it, and I didn't know what to say or do. I went out and bought the book *When Bad Things Happen to Good People* by Harold S. Kushner, a Jewish rabbi. After reading it, I gave it to my grief-stricken friend. It helped both of us.

When Bad Things Happen to Good People

What I learned from that book I have taken forward as a parent and fighter pilot leader. First, the book did not defend or explain God. There is not a religious person I know who has not questioned the fairness or justice of God. Some have even stopped believing in God after having suffered a devastating loss, such as the death of an innocent child. It is a painful, lonely, and frustrating place to be. It produces feelings of guilt, anger, hatred, and bitterness. If you're convinced that God is the cause of your misfortune, then you either conclude that you are being punished for something, given a test of faith, taught a lesson, or made an example of. The book points out an alternative understanding, one that I subscribe to.

Some believe that God tinkers with every detail of every moment of everyone's life in fulfillment of a grand, individualized life plan. I don't believe that's the case. What if God simply created order from chaos, as the book suggests, as an inviolable set of natural laws and relationships that never change over time. They are beautiful in their simplicity and vastness. They are unbiased, indiscriminate, and in constant play, simultaneously creating both beautiful sunsets as well as catastrophic hurricanes.

Additionally, God created humans in His image, with the capability to recognize their own mortality, the freedom of moral choice, and the gift of creativity. Unlike animals that are bound by instinctive, programmed behaviors, humans can override instinct and make decisions that are potentially either constructive or destructive. It is their God-given free will.

With these two dynamics in play, both unbelievably good and bad things can and will happen to both good and bad people. More importantly, despite God's anguish and compassion when bad things happen, changing either natural laws or free will to accommodate some at the

continued

expense of others defeats His creative purpose—namely the freedom to choose to love God.

And although bad things happen to everyone, there are plenty more good things to celebrate. Humans have used their creativity to better understand and harness the laws of nature in order to improve quality of life and better protect each other from the destructive choices that many will make.

As a result of these original creation conditions, as described, it follows that there is no proportionality, moral equivalency, or privileged class when it comes to bad things. Illness, accidents, crime, and natural disasters will happen to everyone. And in the end, everyone dies. Expecting God, who abhors our suffering, to undo what makes us human or to undo nature is outside His plan. Kushner's book suggests that instead of asking, "Why did this bad thing happen to me?" a better question and context would be, "Now that this has happened, what shall I do about it?" This approach focuses on the future, and this is where God can really work for you.

In naval aviation, and particularly in a Navy fighter squadron, the loss of life is all too common. Young men and women are taken in their prime, leaving young families behind to grieve and figure out what to do in the aftermath. In support of these suffering families, I endeavored to apply what I'd learned—now that this has happened, what do I do about it?—from Kushner's book.

Yes, miracles do happen. And when they do, by all means I give credit to God and offer praise and thanks. But I no longer pray for miracles. I focus on the future, and I focus on what God will actually do for me.

The Future Is Where God Does His Best Work

In tragedy, suffering, and threatening situations, sometimes God is the only one available, like in my trusty F/A-18 cockpit. With God, you are not alone in your grief, pain, frustration, or fears. With that partnership going for you, you unleash a reserve of strength, courage, and peace to move forward through any hardship or challenge. God also inspires others to come to your aid to share the burden of your situation and comfort you. God makes sure you are never alone, and He motivates others to resolve the biological, mechanical, engineering, or social factors that contributed to your hardship.

The evolution of humanity is also a history of how horrible things are investigated, understood, and overcome. You can thank God for that as well. In naval aviation, as I discussed earlier, "written in blood" is the term we use to describe how a tragic aviation event is used to protect future pilots from the same situation. The future is where God does His best work. That is where I spend my time with God. That is where I teach my children to focus. In order to help them to better understand their purpose, direct their passion, and persevere through the challenges they will undoubtedly encounter, my most significant contribution has been to connect them to their future via coaches, teachers, professionals, and faith mentors who will share their "written in blood" experiences and guide them along their journey. Equally important, though, is for them to give back by doing the same for others.

When Your Prayers Change

As a result of this new understanding, all my prayers—but especially my cockpit prayers—changed significantly. I stopped asking for the impossible (change something that has already happened), unnatural (a waiver from natural law), revenge, or for God to do something I was capable of doing myself. The first two are fairly easy. Revenge is a little trickier since it involves a strong emotional demand to correct an injustice caused by another human. But I think the last one—asking for God to do something you can do yourself—is where children can use the strongest example and guidance. Achieving a 4.0 grade point average, an athletic scholarship, or acceptance to a dream school or program requires individual hard work, focus, and perseverance. But also recognize that achievement, without going through the controlled failure process, will set you up for future failure. My new prayers, and the example I demonstrate for my children, generally ask for strength, courage, focus, endurance, patience, and composure when dealing with a hardship or an impending challenge. I also ask God to refresh every lesson I've learned while chasing perfection. When I do this, I have never been disappointed. I've been able to beat down fear and perform under intense pressure and stress. I've also learned to appreciate even the smallest things. For my children, this has been a never-ending process applied to every dimension of their life until it became self-sustaining. Now, not only do they know how to draw strength and confidence reserves through faith and prayer, but they are also ready to support others who come up short.

Focus on the Good When There Is Bad

There are many good things happening around us, but it seems as though the bad things get all the attention. By celebrating and appreciating each tiny good and beautiful thing we witness, joy and happiness quickly nudge out anger, despair, and frustration. Hope replaces hopelessness. Happiness replaces discouragement and sadness. Hidden in the news, and in our own daily lives, you will find random acts of kindness, selfless service to others, and stories of those who overcame adversity. From the police officer who bought the homeless man shoes to the person who beat cancer, when you commit to looking for good and beautiful things, no matter how slight, you will find them. These are the important lessons that I share with my kids and upon which I put a premium as a fighter pilot.

A few years after I retired, a close colleague of mine—someone I respected and admired—decided he was going to start flying tactical fighter aircraft again as part of a commercial adversary company. Extremely bored with his post-retirement desk job, he missed flying, he missed speed, and he missed the camaraderie. We had lived next door to each other, we went to the same church, and our career paths were nearly identical.

One fateful day, shortly after he joined his new company, he was flying a mission near Fallon, Nevada (home of Top Gun), in an Israeli-made F-21 Kfir. Not unlike the Hawaii mission I described earlier, many things went wrong. The combination of weather issues, conflicting air traffic, and low fuel conspired to place my friend in an unrecoverable position. Just short of landing, he ran out of gas and was forced to land. Although he got the aircraft on the ground, his speed and trajectory placed him on a path toward a building. Sadly, he didn't survive the impact. A bad thing happened to an extremely good person.

His memorial service and burial ceremony were held at the Fort Rosecrans National Cemetery in San Diego. Not surprisingly, the past and present elite of naval aviation were in attendance. We had all grown up with the all-too-common tragedy of losing friends in the prime of their life and having to console their young, grieving families. We understood that bad things happened to good people, and there was no good explanation for it. We all had sufficient experience to know just how close we had all come to the same fate throughout our own careers. We also understood that by coming together in remembrance and support, we gained strength and perspective, and it helped us do the same for our friend's family. Especially for kids, tragedy and sudden loss should not be suffered in silence and isolation.

At the reception following the burial, it eventually came time for toasts and stories. Every new speaker tried to outperform his predecessors in boldness, respect, and humor while sharing a vignette that was both special and memorable for our fallen comrade, his family, and each other. Tears quickly gave way to rib-popping laughter. It was very clear that what didn't kill us made for very amusing and embarrassing stories. Some of the stories even included flying. I told the story of our last flight together at Top Gun.

The Fine Line Between Glory and Defeat

We had both been simultaneously selected for F/A-18 Squadron Command, and we were also both scheduled to leave Fallon, Nevada, nearly on the same day. Our last flight, a Navy tradition, was also scheduled on the same day and just happened to be a Top Gun 1v1 graduation flight—which happens to be the singularly most fun flight there is.

All types of fighter aircraft and pilots from multiple backgrounds come to Fallon for this one-day air-to-air slugfest. At the brief, each pilot is issued an envelope. On the enclosed piece of paper is his or her call sign (mine was Goon 151), a frequency, a launch time, and coordinates for the start point. The only simulated weapons allowed are an air-to-air gun and an early generation heat-seeking missile. When pilots get to their starting gate, they coordinate on the radio a cooperative neutral intercept. They have no idea who is in the other jet, what type of aircraft they are flying, or what their tactics will be. Most try to disguise their voice and sneak into the merge using the sun or terrain for concealment.

The key to success is seeing the other aircraft first, recognizing what kind of aircraft it is, and putting the proper tactics in play. The uncertainty factor is very much like combat—no one likes to lose. What I didn't know was that my good (and now deceased) friend was also my adversary that day (his call sign was Goon 94).

It is important to point out that both of us had been moving our families in the preceding days. I had driven my family eight hours to Lemoore, California, the previous day and then drove all the way back to give my last training lecture to an air wing going through its advanced pre-deployment syllabus. After my lecture, I collected my remaining things and headed over to my flight brief before my final flight. I had been operating on pure adrenaline for three days, but I was excited to finish up my tour with this event. Immediately after the flight, I was planning on driving back to Lemoore. Goon 94 had similar distractions.

A bunch of us walked to our airplanes at about the same time. I saw my good friend, but it didn't dawn on me at the time that he might be my competition. We launched and arrived at our push points. Disguising our voices, we coordinated our first run. Then we started with our standard transmission: "Fights On, Tapes On, Switches Safe." The adrenaline kicked in.

We quickly closed from our initial twenty-mile separation. After seventy seconds, we had to be close. We saw each other at about the same time. When we passed each other canopy to canopy, we were fairly neutral. We both chose a nose low turn, and when I pulled hard back into him, I began to realize that I wasn't feeling it that day. The last three days had taken their toll. In my weakened condition, I started to get tunnel vision pretty easily with just the slightest amount of g-force.

I had to ease my pull or risk losing consciousness. I figured Goon 94 would quickly take advantage and make angles on me.

He didn't. We were still neutral. After passing each other a couple more times and getting close to our minimum altitude, we knocked it off and set up for a couple more similarly uninspiring engagements. When we finally landed and saw each other without our masks on, we were both sporting slightly embarrassed smiles. It was not our best day. We were much better than what we had just demonstrated, and we also knew that we probably had pushed our limits a little too far.

This story illustrates how parents should use key partnerships to navigate the fine line between glory and catastrophe.

The Persistent Demand on Faith

As I listened to more and more of these stories, two themes emerged. First, in our business, there is a very fine line between good and bad, thrills and scares, glory and defeat. Second, we were highly dependent on one another to navigate that fine line without going over it. And if and when we did, we were highly dependent on one another to work through the potential outcomes that followed. Bad things clearly happened to all of us, but it was amazing to listen to the countless times our now-deceased shipmate had been intimately involved in preventing a lot more from happening to each of us.

Woven into our training, experience, preparation, and education was

> "Kids need God and faith in their lives, or they will eventually fill the void with other things, either disproportionate elements from the other quadrants of their medicine wheel or empty substitutes."

the persistent demand on faith and the support from others when bad things happened. I truly believe that it is important for kids to learn how to keep their medicine wheel in balance, especially the spiritual side. There really is no good substitute. This is where they will find their true strength, courage, focus, endurance, patience, and composure when dealing with a hardship or an impending challenge.

It took me a while, but being a fighter pilot really helped me refine my relationship with God. It helped me to fully appreciate every small blessing. It helped me to optimally manage adversity and tragedy, and it helped me find ways to serve others who were dealing with challenges, especially my kids. Kids need God and faith in their lives, or they will eventually fill the void with other things, either disproportionate elements from the other quadrants of their medicine wheel or empty substitutes. Staying true to their purpose and passion is best served when their medicine wheel is balanced by faith.

Therefore, as a fighter pilot parent, I try to set a faith example for my kids. I share my faith journey and lessons I've learned along the way. You must endeavor to do the same in your own genuine way. I share what I pray for, and I remind my kids how special they are and how much God loves them . . . no matter what.

★★★

 ## FIGHTER PILOT PARENT TAKEAWAYS— About Faith Principles

★ Parents and children are designed to worship something bigger than themselves.

★ Make sure spirituality is a part of the balance between the

physical, emotional/social, and wisdom/intellectual pursuits
of children.

★ Meet God halfway, ask for help, be content with what you have,
give in faith, be honest, and trust Him.

★ Don't ask God for the impossible (to change something that has
already happened), unnatural (a waiver from natural law), for
revenge, or to do something you're capable of doing yourself.

★ Concentrate your children's prayers on strength, courage, focus,
endurance, patience, and composure—and to refresh every lesson
they've learned.

CHAPTER THREE

CHARACTER, INTEGRITY, AND ETHICAL COURAGE

———

When it comes to critical and essential personal attributes, it is my opinion that any investment you make to advance your talents—without having a strong foundation of high character, integrity, and ethical courage—is a worthless pursuit. You need to be able to lead yourself before you can lead others. In the dynamic world of human relationships, trust matters. In the world of fighter pilots, as in many other professions, it is the *only* thing that matters. Everyone wants to be trusted and respected, but only the very best take the time to put in the effort. Trust can't be bought, and it can't be borrowed. Trust can only be earned, and the journey starts with the mastery of self-leadership, where your commitment in action to an inspirational set of beliefs and values is nonnegotiable.

What is so important and magical about trust? Simply put, trust is the key that unlocks the foundational elements of leadership: respect, loyalty, and even obedience. Without it, you become marginalized and ineffective as a leader or a parent. Opportunities dissipate. Success becomes harder to achieve. This is true in the air; it's also true in parenting. When you lose trust, you set that standard for others to follow.

The military, especially the Navy, understands this dynamic and places its highest value on these key personal attributes when selecting commanders. There is no tolerance for even the perception of compromise when it comes to character, integrity, and courage deficiencies.

I wish our political elite class held the same high standard as the military. I used to tell all my new personnel during check-in that they would be held to a higher professional standard than even our commander in chief. Politics don't exist or matter when missiles and anti-air artillery are targeting you.

Unfortunately, it has become increasingly more common for elected officials to take character and integrity waivers when policy or personal power objectives get in the way. From the public's perspective, our "leadership" just doesn't seem to have any shame, and no one seems to hold anyone accountable anymore. Sadly, even voters contribute to a lower expectation for political character by perpetually returning clearly flawed candidates back to office. Politician favorability ratings, especially in Congress, demonstrate the corrosive effect of low character and integrity over time. Today trust in government is at an all-time low.

Unfortunately, the Navy can make mistakes in their leadership selection process, too, but their response is very different from what happens in civilian life. Each year somewhere between twenty and thirty commanders are prematurely relieved of their duties. In nearly every case, loss of confidence is the publicly cited trip wire. This phrase could mean many things, but generally speaking, compromises in character and integrity are typically at play. In other words, trust was broken.

In 2015, nineteen Navy commanders, four executive officers, and eight command master chiefs (senior enlisted representatives) were relieved of their duties following thorough investigations. Here are some of the descriptions of their shortcomings:

☆ loss of confidence in their ability to lead/command

☆ inappropriate behavior

☆ toxic command climate

☆ mistreatment of a sailor

☆ poor judgment, failure to meet and uphold the highest personal and professional standards, and poor program management

☆ professional shortcomings

☆ personal misconduct

☆ misuse of government funds

☆ improper hiring practices

☆ sexual harassment

I am inspired by the high standard the military sets for their personnel and feel blessed to have been cultivated in an organization that places such high value on these essential qualities. It should therefore be no surprise that the US military enjoys the highest public confidence of any institution in the US. Why? Because character, integrity, and courage actually mean something in that world. It has to, because it often means life and death on the battlefield and in the air.

It is no different when it involves your kids.

Where Courage Comes In

How do you develop these qualities in yourself? How do you develop these qualities in your kids? It's a process, and it doesn't happen accidentally. Character and integrity are taught, demonstrated, incentivized, and allowed to mature over time. Personal accountability is never delegated and never deflected when failures occur. And since character and integrity are behaviors, those behaviors have to become habits and routines that drive every decision and response—no matter who is watching or what the consequences are.

In our home, we are quick to acknowledge and celebrate notable examples of high character and integrity made by public leaders, celebrities, friends, classmates, teammates, and especially each other. We also take note when those same people fail, applying a special emphasis on the long-term consequences of character and integrity compromise by asking this simple question: "Would you ever trust them in the future?"

Character and Integrity Have Persistent Enemies

This direct emotional inflection point combined with an environment that places character and integrity above lesser priorities helps create the proper spirit to fight through all the common pressures that would lead a young person to falter. So as obviously wonderful as these qualities are, why does it seem so hard for people of all ages to embrace them? It's simple: Character and integrity have persistent enemies— pride, ego, popularity, competition, time, cost, and convenience. That is where courage comes in, and teenagers are especially vulnerable when it comes to popularity and fitting in with their peers. At least mine were.

Without courage, character and integrity won't stand a chance. It is the counterforce to those enemies. Think about it for a second. How refreshing is it to hear someone accept responsibility for a mistake and then apologize or even resign? That takes courage. Despite the mistake, we commend the person and are inspired by the virtuous conduct. Mistakes, bad decisions, and poor performance are always going to happen in an imperfect world. Sacrificing character and integrity—alongside the failure—is not a good response. The cover-up or denial will only serve to delay correcting the mistake and will guarantee more frequent and severe integrity compromises in the future. When you squander your character and integrity, there is no getting it back. And remember—trust, loyalty, character, integrity, and high first-time success all travel in the same pack. Where one goes, the others follow.

Tough Decisions and Responsibility for the Behavior of Others

I've witnessed exemplary courageous acts throughout my career, but there is one example that stands out to this day. It is the story I think about when I'm faced with a tough decision or when someone I'm responsible for makes a mistake, because it illustrates the most critical leadership attribute. It started on board the USS *Kitty Hawk* just prior to a Hong Kong port visit in 1993.

Things were going well, and morale was high. We were almost flying too much, if that was even possible. And we were about to pull into one of the greatest cities in the world. All we had to do was build up a little night landing currency so we could enjoy our port visit and still have a sufficient number of night-current pilots when we pulled back out. To make it all happen, we had to work really hard for a few days. We increased the sortie rate to a slightly uncomfortable level and extended the normal fly day by a few hours. The weather was great, and it was fun and professionally rewarding to be flying at a pace we hadn't experienced for a few weeks.

On the last day before our port visit as we were in the process of transitioning to night operations, we positioned our first group of night aircraft in sequence behind the ship's catapults and were preparing to launch. As is our normal process, I went to Air Operations, the ship's module where all aircraft operations are managed, as the designated F/A-18 representative for the first night event. I met with the representatives of the other airplanes flying that night and we prepared resources should an emergency occur during launch or recovery. I took note of the pilots' names and aircraft side numbers and then relaxed while chatting with the other reps about our pending port visit plans. The first aircraft up for launch, an F/A-18, was ready on catapult two, but it would have to wait another five minutes until the ship completed its turn into the wind.

Like clockwork, the F/A-18 from our sister squadron (the term we use when there are two squadrons flying the same type aircraft) slowly maneuvered his jet forward, lining up perfectly with the catapult two track until his launch bar (a metal arm that lowers from the nose wheel) mated to the ship's catapult shuttle (the actual part of the catapult system that pulls the aircraft forward) as the ship steadied on the final launch heading. We dimmed the lights in Air Ops and got our game faces on. The jet blast deflector (JBD), a large "wall" that elevates behind a launching aircraft to protect others from its powerful exhaust, came up behind the aircraft, and in moments the entire ship started vibrating as the pilot advanced his throttles to afterburner, a common feature on fighter aircraft where fuel is ignited in the section aft of the normal engines for additional thrust. On the F/A-18, this is recognized by a bright blue plume, similar to a water heater pilot light, extending several feet behind the aircraft. After cycling his controls, the pilot received a thumbs-up from all safety observers. It was now up to him. He examined his instruments, positioned his body, and then turned on his external lights to signal he was ready for launch.

When the lights came on, the catapult officer responded and pressed the button to release steam into the catapult. The jet's nose squatted as the shuttle began its trek forward. I had watched thousands of catapults, and something seemed immediately out of place. It took me a moment before I recognized exactly what was different. Right after the catapult fired, I could see a gradually increasing spray of sparks mixing with the bright blue afterburner plume. I leaned forward and shared my concern with the Air Operations team. I wasn't the only one. Others watching commented over the launch radio frequency.

Although airborne now, the jet wasn't climbing, and the exhaust sparks persisted. The pilot was staying uncomfortably low, despite being directed to climb multiple times. I knew it wasn't as if he didn't want to; for some reason he couldn't comply. After a long period of silence, the pilot finally transmitted that he was having problems with both engines. As the F/A-18 rep on duty, I turned and opened up my trusty F/A-18 emergency book. I scanned the sections for engine malfunctions as I took a seat next to the radio so I could talk to him. He jettisoned his fuel tanks (4,000 pounds of gas), which offered some relief, but he was still only a few hundred feet off the water. When his engines started coughing and vibrating, he had had enough. At approximately three miles ahead of the ship, he reached for the handle between his legs and initiated ejection. One problem was solved, but another one—a big one—was looming.

An aircraft carrier is a big ship. It covers a lot of ocean when it turns or tries to stop. When a mishap occurs during a launch or recovery, all remaining launches are terminated, landing aircraft are sent into a holding pattern, and the ship will turn, slow down, or stop to best accommodate a rescue. If a pilot has the misfortune of ejecting in front of the ship during launch, there is a strong possibility that the ship will continue toward him no matter how hard it turns or tries to stop. Seventy thousand tons takes a long time to redirect.

The unfortunate pilot, having safely ejected from his stricken jet, was now treading water in the China Sea and going through his water survival procedures. When he turned to get his bearings, he was likely very surprised to see a dark monstrosity bearing down on him. The possibility of being run over by an aircraft carrier had not been covered in our survival training. He furiously tried to backstroke to safety but didn't seem to be generating much distance between him and the giant ship. His primary concern was not so much getting hit by the ship as it was getting sucked up in the saltwater intakes the ship uses for cooling and making fresh water.

As the ship came closer and closer, the pilot positioned his feet for impact with the intent of pushing off the side. This tactic worked pretty well, and he continued down the ship's side into clear water for what ended up being a routine helicopter rescue. With the pilot safe, it was now time to find out what went wrong with his plane.

When both jet engines simultaneously spark and fail, it usually means they have sucked something up on the flight deck during catapult that has caused catastrophic damage to both engines. The ship's crew and the air wing work tirelessly to prevent this from happening by conducting meticulous flight deck visual inspections prior to launch. The catapult area had just been inspected. As the investigative focus immediately centered on the flight deck forward of the catapult, the culprit—lots of tiny round steel ball bearings—was found. These bearings were the same kind normally found in an S-3 Viking nose tire.

When the investigation team reviewed the crashed jet's maintenance records, the only maintenance performed before the fateful flight was a nose-wheel tire change. The mystery was solved: They had replaced an F/A-18 nose tire with an S-3 tire. How could this have happened? Well, the tires were basically the same size and the S-3 could easily fit on an F/A-18 nose strut. In a rush to make sure the jet would be flying in the next scheduled takeoff and not lose a precious sortie, the maintenance crew made several mistakes. Visually, especially at night, it was hard to tell the difference between the two wheels, except for a slight gap that existed after it was mounted. It was no big deal to taxi in that condition, but as soon as the tire spun up during catapult, the bearings spewed out and bounced off the flight deck, where the two motors, operating at full power, immediately sucked them up. Engine death quickly followed. Like most mishaps, it was due to human failure.

I was thankful it wasn't my squadron that was involved. There is no bigger morale killer than to lose a jet—unless you lose the pilot too. And although they were my sister squadron—a friendly competitor—I was really beside myself. I loved them like the brothers they were, and I felt horrible for them. I knew the technicians who were directly involved, and I had the highest respect for them. If they were football players, they'd have been drafted in the first round. The squadron commander was my personal hero and had taken over the squadron that same day. It was literally his first day in office, and his formal ceremony was scheduled the very next day on the foc'sle, a large open area on an aircraft carrier where the massive anchor chains flow through as the anchors extend or retract. I thought to myself, *This is going to be a very awkward change of command.*

The change of command ceremony proceeded as planned. At the end, the new commanding officer (CO) spoke. It is considered polite and professional to keep the ceremony to forty-five minutes and minimize the new CO's speaking duration—five minutes of targeted gratitude is about right.

But when it was his turn to speak, the big "mishap elephant" was still in the room. It hadn't been mentioned at all. All that was about to change.

True Character

As we expected, the typical distribution of praise and thanks led his speech. Then there was a long, awkward pause. What he said next was the most powerful public display of character, integrity, and courage I had ever witnessed.

In my recollection, he said something like this: "This squadron lost an aircraft, and nearly a pilot, yesterday. It was completely and totally my fault. Following my aggressive lead and my demand for flawless sortie completion, I let my sailors down. In their eagerness to fulfill my objectives, shortcuts were taken. I let them down. Their shortcuts were mine. I will never let that happen again. This squadron and the great men who serve it deserve better, and that is exactly what I intend to give them as their new CO."

His powerful message impacted both the attitude and trajectory of this squadron. Morale and professional pride changed instantaneously. There was no one in that audience who didn't want to be in that squadron or be led by that CO. Why? The character, integrity, and ethical courage he demonstrated now defined who they were as a team.

Honesty and accountability were embraced and celebrated. That guy had their collective backs.

"People who have developed strong character, integrity, and courage traits tend to have deep remorse when they make a mistake and let the team down."

His example didn't just begin in that moment; it had been forged over years through continuous example and reinforcement. It was incentivized and rewarded. As parents, that is what we also should strive to do. But he also recognized that men and women of high character and integrity take failure harder than anyone else, and they need to be absolved, so to speak, before they can truly recover and move forward. His speech was really part of that process.

People who have developed strong character, integrity, and courage traits tend to have deep remorse when they make a mistake and let the team down. In some cases, the only way they can shake it off and get back into the game is to get involved with the mitigation, correction, or remedy. They also make the team part of the solution, and thereby the team serves a penance of sorts. This impressed upon me that character and integrity development should also include what I like to call a "return to glory" feature following absolution.

Hard Landings and Overstress

Since failure is a natural human fixture, even men and women of high character and integrity will fail sometimes. The only difference between them and other people is how they deal with it. There are two common areas where pilots frequently fail the team and feel miserable afterward: hard landings and overstress.

The F/A-18 is a wonderful machine that has served the Navy well. It tells you when it is sick, and it tells you when it has been abused. Pilots dread seeing two main "abuse" maintenance codes: a 904 code indicates that the plane has suffered a hard landing, and an 811 code indicates an overstress. When these codes are generated, the jet is taken off the flight schedule, and intrusive abuse inspections ensue. The pilot, in addition to his professional embarrassment at having caused the codes, also feels guilty for the extra work he or she has caused. Both of these abuse codes are not uncommon when chasing fighter pilot perfection. As part of my return to glory strategy, I decided I needed a way to absolve these dejected pilots while preserving the seriousness of their failure. I looked to the Air Force for an option.

Shooting Down a Friendly Teammate

In the fighter pilot training arena, there is no greater sin than shooting down a "friendly" or "blue" teammate. The term used for such a thing is a "blue-on-blue." When chasing perfection, this will occasionally occur in training. Fortunately, real missiles aren't being exchanged. The only thing worse than shooting down another colleague during training is shooting down your wingman, particularly if he is your CO. In the Air Force, the perpetrator of such an egregious training offense is obliged to buy a keg of beer for the offended squadron or air wing. In this return to glory process, everyone learns a lesson, the pilot is absolved, and refreshments are free. It is a powerful performance motivator and offers some much-needed absolution for men and women of character and integrity.

Now back to my situation. How did I free my pilots of the self-loathing they felt after abusing one of our precious war fighting assets? Buy a keg? No, but sort of. Their penance was to observe the "post-abuse" inspection process, acknowledge the names of the technicians who performed the work to repair the abuse, and contribute, if willing, twenty dollars to the next squadron party. No one was excused from this policy. I also observed inspections and contributed forty dollars from time to time myself. Being a senior officer, the fine was double for me, but the absolution was well worth it.

No Greater Failure

The F/A-18 abuse codes bring up other important factors in developing strong character, integrity, and courage: oversight and feedback. In the early stages of character and integrity development, and sometimes even in later stages, courage seems to be the weak link. People generally know right from wrong but fail to commit to the actions that back up their inspirational beliefs and values. To get to the stage that it becomes automatic, sometimes developing that courage component requires conditioning. This is a delicate process. How do you detect a character or integrity breech and nudge a person back to a good courage posture without losing them?

With kids, it starts by drawing the contrast between two distinct character and integrity options and making sure the potential consequences always bend favorably toward the higher side. It finishes with putting your money where your mouth is. Make doing the right thing feel that way. Ultimately, kids need to feel that there is no greater failure than compromising their own character and integrity. But this is not a natural response. It has to be learned through practice and a strong and supporting environment. Ethical courage must always be rewarded, even when failures occur. Over time, commitment in action—doing the right thing—becomes automatic—as if we assume we are always being videotaped.

I remember seeing a World War II film clip where a general (I think it was Lieutenant General Holland Smith, a brilliant World War II Island Campaign commander, but I can't confirm this) said, "There are no cowards in front of a camera." The same is true with respect to character and integrity flaws. The general was so convinced that he would send videographers into battle even if they didn't have any film. I agree with him 100 percent. It works like magic in developing ethical courage.

I tell younger pilots that the two most important developments in naval aviation were the two cameras that were mounted in the F/A-18, over our shoulders, in the mid-'90s. They were called elbow cameras, and they recorded all our tactical cockpit displays and communications. The aforementioned blue-on-blues, hard landings, and overstresses were recorded and analyzed. We also penalized anyone who failed to record their flight, and we considered that failure a serious professional breech that would not be tolerated. Now, in the modern air warfare environment where rules of engagement are so strict, video recordings are essential, if only to prove you did the right thing. This is where I learned the value of transparency when it came to character, integrity, and courage. When you know that everything you do professionally is recorded, there is an extra incentive and motivation to perform at your best and be honest about your performance when you don't quite get there. I literally watched naval aviation change overnight when there was no longer any escape from the tough and honest critique that film provided.

Over time this behavioral shift and ethical courage conditioning eventually turned into good habits and routines that led to very strong character and integrity traits in all areas—and a stronger commitment in action to honor them. For parenting, the elbow cameras could just as easily be any form of proper supervision, chaperones, or due diligence (trust but verify). As parents we can set the most powerful example by being the hardest on ourselves and avoiding the "do as I say, not as I do" tendency.

> "As parents we can set the most powerful example by being the hardest on ourselves and avoiding the 'do as I say, not as I do' tendency."

After each training or combat mission, we watched every tape and listened to everyone's communications. Good leaders and teachers set the tone by meticulously nitpicking their own mistakes, thus creating the optimal environment for learning. The tapes certified the obvious. Pride and ego were disarmed. We saw that everyone made mistakes, and everyone could learn from those mistakes. As a result, everyone learned more quickly, and everyone became quite comfortable with honest critique. It also saved a lot of time and money.

Before the cameras arrived, tactical failures were often blamed on equipment degrades, especially the radar. The technicians would swap boxes and run tests and usually never quite find a smoking gun. Countless hours were wasted, and parts were needlessly replaced, at great cost, chasing down these phantom problems.

The cameras, however, told a completely different story. As we would soon discover, it was rarely the equipment's fault. Most problems originated either at the pilot's fingertips or in the six-inch space between the pilot's ears. The excuses (which were the equivalent of "the dog ate my homework") for not finding targets on radar could no longer be blamed on the radar. The eventual savings in replacement part costs and troubleshooting time were significant. The cameras also eviscerated pride, ego, competitive posturing, and self-aggrandizement. What an amazing return on investment!

Enhancing Character and Integrity Building

In parenting—as in developing the most capable fighter pilots—incentivizing and being honest and open about continuous behavior and decision-making improvement will inevitably lead to better habits and routines that directly enhance character and build integrity. It's a priceless process.

Rules Are for the Other Guys

Between 1984 and 1991, I had the interesting experience of being part of the most mishap-prone air wing in the terminal phase of the Cold

War. It seemingly had an unshakeable curse. Sure, we did a lot of high-risk things in preparation for a hot war with a nuclear power, but so did all the other air wings. Why were we different? Why couldn't we shake this? Some examples of our troubles:

☆ On Halloween night 1985, just prior to our first deployment, my ship, the USS *Enterprise*, ran aground on Bishop Rock, off San Clemente Island, California, as we were trying to avoid a fog bank.

☆ On our actual first day of deployment, January 28, 1986 (the same day as the Challenger Space Shuttle disaster), an F-14 crew ejected themselves (without being strapped into their seats) as they were trying to retrieve a variety of unauthorized cockpit items that had been displaced during their landing. Both crew members shot forty to fifty feet in the air and fell back to the flight deck to their deaths.

☆ Within a week of the first incident, an A-7 departed from controlled flight—a condition where the aircraft is basically free-falling and unresponsive to control input—while training for air-to-air combat. The pilot was forced to eject, but survived and was rescued.

☆ Next up—and not more than a week after the second incident—an A-7 and its junior maintenance person in the cockpit while the aircraft was being repositioned for the next launch rolled backward off the ship's edge. The maintenance person's body was never found.

☆ Within the month, disaster would strike again. As we approached an area where Soviet bombers would frequently try to find deploying aircraft carriers, we started an aggressive intercept program targeting 500-plus miles for intercept and escort. The F-14 Tomcat was our primary tool. To protect the ship, we turned all electronic emissions off. Everything was going pretty smoothly until our last airborne F-14 transmitted, "Go active." This meant turning everything on so they could find the ship. We complied, but we still couldn't locate them, nor could they locate us. In great detail, they described where they thought they were, their gradual depletion of fuel, and their ejection. Then we lost all contact with them.

It took four days, a massive search with no good starting point, and a lucky visual sighting, but we finally found them alive—500 miles from where they thought they were, floating in their rafts in the ocean. In their rush to launch on a real threat, their navigation systems were not fully synchronized, and they completed the process en route to their first intercept. Although it is perfectly safe and common to complete the process en route, they mistakenly entered the winds into their system, using the 180-degree opposite direction. After several hours, the navigation error grew exponentially, driving them on a vector that took them out of radar range. Surprisingly, their radio transmissions were efficiently ducted (an air mass phenomenon that extends the range of radio frequency energy), such that the ship was left with the impression that they were a lot closer.

☆ Even my commanding officer was not immune to our seeming curse. After completing his approach turn and leveling his wings for a day landing, his throttle didn't work. There was no response. He safely ejected at flight deck level and was quickly recovered. The jet landed next to the ship and floated for a while with its single vertical stabilizer visible above the waterline like a shark fin. The throttle linkage had failed. This was one of the few mishaps I've seen where human error was not a causal factor.

☆ And finally, to wrap up the deployment, during an EA-6B Prowler launch, one of the massive cockpit instruments that slide into a sleeve just forward of the control stick dislodged during catapult, pinning the controls full aft. As the jet's nose quickly went straight up, it ran out of airspeed, and all four crew members were forced to eject. The ones that landed on the flight deck received significant injuries and those that landed in the water were injury-free. The maintenance department had failed to screw in the instrument display after they had replaced it.

I left the air wing and eventually came back to it on a different ship as the Landing Signal and Safety officer. What did I return to? The helicopter that dropped me off on the new ship—the USS *Abraham Lincoln*—crashed on its following mission. Two F-14s ran into each other; one went into the sea, while the other landed in Singapore. An F-14's wings failed to reposition properly during transition for landing, and the pilot had to eject. And an F/A-18 launched with the wrong catapult setting, which didn't provide enough airspeed, and the pilot was forced to eject.

Things didn't change when we returned from deployment.

☆ An F/A-18 departed from controlled flight during a routine air combat training mission in an aircraft that was not properly configured for that mission.

☆ Another F/A-18 flew into the ground on an unauthorized low-altitude mission.

☆ An S-3 departed from controlled flight while performing unauthorized maneuvers.

☆ An A-6 flew into a crop duster on an authorized training mission and an authorized low-altitude training route. Additionally, we learned later that one of the crew should never have been flying in the first place; he had forged his own medical certificate, indicating a total lack of character and integrity.

There were many more mishaps after I left, but I'll stop here. The point is that culture corruption starts with character compromise, flexible integrity, and mission creep beyond competency borders. There were persistent themes for all but the most purely mechanical failure mishap—one of them being "Rules are for the other guys." Shortcuts for "operational necessity" became the norm, and gross mission creep was rampant. Aircrew who weren't trained or proficient for certain missions, such as air-to-air combat, were doing it anyhow, often in aircraft that weren't designed for those missions.

Preventing a Culture of Mishaps

How could this culture of mishaps be so pervasive? How could such a culture be reversed? After agonizing over these questions for many years, I've concluded that the culture came down to organizational character, integrity, and courage—or a lack thereof. That culture had been insidiously handed down from generation to generation like a bad virus. During that time period, this air wing was rich with great leaders and men of high character. They were also under a great deal of scrutiny as the mishaps piled up, which should have made them even higher performers. What more could they have done? Another EA-6B Prowler mishap ended up being the final straw.

The air wing was closed down for over a month. That was a first. Some of the leaders were fired. Every training, safety, and maintenance process was reviewed in depth. Any incentive that may have existed for taking shortcuts, "fabricating official records," waiving any rules, or operating out of respective mission lanes was neutered. The way they had controlled failure in pursuit of perfection was recalibrated and reconstituted with character, integrity, and courage at its very foundation.

With regard to parenting, the biggest lesson I learned from this experience is that when you compromise character and integrity, no matter how slightly, the speed of the compromise will escalate, and when it does, it will quickly replace doing the right thing at an alarming pace. What's worse—once not doing the right thing is out of the bottle, it is hard to get it back in.

Most Kids Know Right from Wrong, but . . .

By now, I hope you are starting to understand my general approach to developing honorable children with their character and integrity intact. I believe that most people and most kids know right from wrong. And I think that most kids try to make good choices in their daily lives. But even if they know right from wrong and are trying to make good choices, something can always go wrong.

As a veteran parent of teenagers, I was really taken aback when I was confronted with an unexpected pattern of deceit and potentially high-risk behavior from my formerly model children. The simultaneous pressures of puberty, fitting in, popularity, and relationships can overwhelm the teenage senses. Sometimes it can happen in very big ways. To this day, there is no feeling quite like the one you have when you can't find your child, even if they are seventeen years old—or older!

At the end of a normal school day, my daughter failed to return home from high school swimming practice. She was driving my twenty-year-old Jeep Cherokee, and I assumed she might have been experiencing problems with it. We tried calling her, but she didn't answer. I got in my car and scouted the routes she would normally take home, to no avail, while my wife contacted the coach. Then things got worse: The coach told us there hadn't been any practice that day. Now what?

We called the local hospitals and provided the license plate number to the highway patrol to see if there had been any accidents. Thankfully there was no match. My wife called my daughter's friends, and they could offer no help either. Now it was getting late. I found myself driving around all the places she might go and examining every car that went by me. With each minute that passed, my anxiety increased.

Just as I was about to call the police, my wife called to let me know that she was in contact with our daughter and that someone would be dropping her off at school. As I waited at school, a truck approached. It stopped. I got out of my car to talk to the driver but the truck sped away as soon as my daughter jumped out.

Who Was She with and Where Was My Jeep?

At least she was all right, but where had she been, who had she been with, and where was my Jeep?

I was about to learn that the Jeep was disabled and had to be abandoned twenty miles away in a seedy part of Van Nuys, California. My daughter had planned to use the cover of swimming practice to meet up with her friend and some of her friends, thinking they could still be back in time to tell us how hard swimming practice had been. Unfortunately, the Jeep didn't cooperate. It turns out it was still very loyal to me.

"I used to think that everyone (even children) had a justification for making a decision and then acting on it. Right?"

I took my daughter with me to help locate my precious Jeep and discovered that the serpentine belt had failed, leaving it lifeless. I made my daughter pay for the tow and the repairs with her summer job savings, and she lost all car privileges for a while. Relieved that she was safe, I finally calmed down and asked the most important question: why?

Whenever I ask my kids why they did something they knew was wrong, the response seems to always be, "I don't know."

"What do you mean, you don't know?"

I used to think that everyone (even children) had a justification for making a decision and then acting on it. Right?

Courage Capacity: One Size Doesn't Fit All

Well, I'm now of the opinion that children have insufficient courage to articulate their reasons. Each of my four kids has a different courage capacity and risk tolerance, not unlike fighter pilots. Knowing those unique differences is essential when creating a safe and healthy environment for each of them to develop and practice good character, integrity, and ethical courage habits. One size doesn't fit all. And as parents, we have a much different risk capacity and tolerance for our children than they have for themselves. As they become older, they will naturally push parent risk thresholds—sometimes dangerously so—without the wisdom or experience to manage those risks.

"Credibility is everything. You have to walk the walk."

This is where fighter pilot parenting comes in. Controlled failure builds experience and wisdom while helping align parent and child risk perspective. This is a never-ending process requiring constant calibration as kids develop and mature. In my daughter's case, we had to revisit her controlled failure process by restricting access to transportation, verifying her whereabouts, and defining zero tolerance behaviors and consequences.

From the parenting perspective, instilling courage in your children is the most challenging task you can face as a parent. If they are highly susceptible to pride, ego, convenience, popularity, and fitting-in pressures, you must be a partner in their courage battles until it becomes self-sustaining for them. I can remember once discovering that at least two of our children had taken candy without paying for it from the grocery store. We were still in the store's parking lot, so instead of ignoring it, I walked them back into the store and had them apologize for the theft and pay for the candy. To some people, my actions toward my children at that moment may seem petty, but the courage partnering process should have no threshold. Lowering standards, giving a pass, or ignoring failures never advances the cause. In fact, it invites more courage compromises. Credibility is everything. You have to walk the walk.

Are you the parent who can take the blame and be accountable for the actions of those who depend on you—or yourself?

Are you the parent who makes the right choices despite the potential consequences?

Are you the parent who celebrates truth and honesty?

Are your behaviors and intentions transparent to your children? Do they convey character, integrity, and courage?

Kids are smart, and they are observant. They know when you make up a story to get out of doing something you committed to or to avoid responsibility for something that didn't go quite right. They know when you take credit for something you didn't do. And they know when your standards shift.

What if there was a camera over their shoulder every time they went out on their own? How would you use it? What would you do if you found something disturbing? I'm certain my daughter never would have contemplated doing what she did had she known it would not go unnoticed.

Another daughter was successfully targeted by an online predator, but she didn't understand how to stop what was happening. Thankfully, we discovered the situation and were able to step in. In both incidents we focused on their courage failure and looked at ways to improve transparency between us when our children are the most vulnerable. In the age of technology and smartphones, it's not that hard. You can monitor their postings, their locations, their conversations, and their friends. You can monitor their internet traffic, and you can also place limits on the sites they visit.

Courage Partnering

Having endured two unfortunate incidents in our family, we have made active participation in our children's social media environment into a system of mutual support, protection, and courage partnering. In this day and age, we can no longer consider this intrusive or controlling; it's imperative that our kids know they can and will be monitored. Conversely, as parents, we subject ourselves to the same scrutiny too. Trust but verify. Remember, there are no cowards and no character flaws when you know you are being recorded by those you respect and don't want to disappoint.

There is no complete set of rules to minimal-risk parenting, but over time, good habits and routines will form, especially when observed behaviors are properly critiqued, rewarded when deserved, and the possibility of absolution exists. Sometimes, though, stronger partnering methods may be needed.

In aviation, as in parenting, controlling the environment and the direct influences on behavior and decision-making may be warranted. In some cases, I would frequently pair struggling pilots with proven mentors and teachers, and I would modify their training environment to be consistent with their current maturity level.

I do the same thing for my kids. There are some friends and families I won't let my kids be around. Therefore, I don't let my kids go to anyone's house without meeting their parents first. It's nothing personal; we might not approach character and integrity the same way they do. And as a general rule, I'm of the opinion that people of low character try to subvert those with higher standards, especially when their courage reserve is not very strong.

"Don't leave (your kids') character and integrity to chance. Your efforts will pay off throughout their lives."

Thankfully there are plenty of friends and parents that subscribe to the same standards, and we are blessed with their partnership. If possible, you should seek out like-minded parents. You can't send your kids out and hope for the best without 100 percent certainty that they have the courage to match the challenges that await them. Parenting demands due diligence, so you can always assist with the courage gaps kids face every day as they develop. Don't leave their character and integrity to chance. Your efforts will pay off throughout their lives. That will be your legacy to them and their children long after you're gone.

No Character and Integrity Waivers

As I bring this chapter to a close, I keep asking myself why people don't get it. They love to be trusted, and they love people they can trust. No one enjoys being deceived, especially by someone in authority or someone they love. Most people despise corruption and want the guilty to be punished. And most people want those who are responsible for mistakes and failures to be held accountable. And yet most people still give themselves character and integrity waivers when it comes to their own self-interests.

We have all experienced a friend or colleague canceling an important planned event, citing a justifiable and noble reason—sickness, for example—only to discover that they were doing something completely different. That constitutes a character waiver. They evidently would much rather avoid the emotional awkwardness of telling you the truth. Character and integrity don't work like that. To have both, you can never give it away. It is not circumstantial or reserved for special people or moments. It is a way of life that requires continuous investment and nurturing.

Even at this stage in my life, I still face tough choices and decisions. Thankfully, I have had the benefit of a career that truly demonstrated and reinforced the tangible and intangible benefits of strong character, uncompromising integrity, and a decisive courage foundation. I lean heavily on that foundation all the time, and it is the single most important quality I want for my kids. From there, good judgment, good decision-making, and optimal performance will flow.

When it comes down to it, the benefits are long lasting and meaningful. I couldn't imagine losing the respect of my family, friends, or colleagues as the result of an integrity or character failure. Conversely, when I see deficiencies in others, I steer clear and then warn others I care about to do the same. Since I've been heavily involved in youth sports over the years, I frequently make coaching recommendations and provide warnings based primarily on character and integrity factors. This extends into business as well.

And finally, character, integrity, and courage are essential for good leadership. You can't lead others until you can lead yourself, which is the commitment in action to an inspiring set of beliefs and core values.

✯✯✯

FIGHTER PILOT PARENT TAKEAWAYS— Character, Integrity, and Ethical Courage

☆ There is no complete set of rules to minimal-risk parenting.

☆ Don't leave your kids' character and integrity to chance.

☆ Trust but verify. It's OK to monitor your kids on social media.

☆ When people of high character and integrity fail, they are extremely hard on themselves. Be mindful of this when your children are trying hard to grow into the people you want them to be.

☆ Be the best example you can be.

☆ Make use of your own strong character, uncompromising integrity, and a decisive courage foundation to instill inspirational beliefs, values, and norms in your kids.

CHAPTER FOUR

LEADERSHIP—IT'S ALL ABOUT SERVICE

When I was first commissioned, one of my biggest concerns was how I would be regarded as a leader. Would I be respected? Would I inspire loyalty? Would I make good decisions? Would I be followed? And that was just on the ground. Airborne leadership seemed like another animal.

As a fighter pilot, I knew things happened fast. I also knew that I would typically be flying in groups of two or four aircraft—sections or divisions, as we call them in the Navy. So, my first exposure to airborne leadership training was learning how to be a good wingman—in other words, to be a good follower.

A good wingman is always in the right place. A good wingman is always up the right radio frequency. A good wingman backs up the flight lead with navigation and emergency procedures. And a good wingman is always ready to take the lead. For both the wingman and the flight lead to be successful, both require a common understanding of the mission and objectives and how they are going to deal with adversity, challenges, and opportunities.

You learn a lot about great leadership at high speeds and in situations of high complexity. Not only do you need to think far ahead of your own jet and weapon systems, but you also need to think ahead of the pilots in your flight as well. Early in my naval aviation experience, I learned that I had to be a good follower before I could be a good leader. And unique to military aviation, if I couldn't lead in the air, I had no chance of earning the respect required to lead on the ground.

On my very first flight in my very first operational squadron, a unit destined for combat, I had the opportunity to fly with the squadron commander. That's scary for a nugget. He was a legend and highly regarded in the community. I didn't know what to expect, but I was warned to stay in tight formation. His preflight brief was simple—a classic example of Vietnam-era "coolness." My recollection is it went something like this: "Join up, shut up, KILL, call in, off, hung, lead, you're on fire, and don't say eject. Any questions?" That was short for "Get in position; don't talk on the radio; execute your mission; let me know when you are rolling in on the target; let me know if your bombs didn't come off; let me know if you see anything wrong with my jet; and don't tell me to eject—I'll decide for myself."

"A good wingman is always in the right place."

Even though I was bursting with questions, I calmly answered, "No, sir." We launched from our home base in Lemoore, California, and I glued myself to his side. His transmissions were minimal, as I expected. As we entered our training airspace, we started maneuvering. It began with acrobatics. We did wingovers and aileron rolls. Then we did loops, half-Cuban eights, and some other high g-force work. As I focused on staying right in place, I could see the rare hand signals he would provide just in advance of the next series of maneuvers. I started to feel my confidence build as I hung in there for each move.

As the flight continued, I began to realize that it wasn't my pilot skills keeping me in position as much as his leadership skill. He was unbelievably smooth with his stick and throttle. He anticipated my reaction time and made timely adjustments to make it easier for me. He gave me just enough information to anticipate what we were going to do next. He gradually increased the level of difficulty when he was satisfied that I could hack it. The last thing we did is something I have never done in tight formation since. We pulled our noses up until they were purely vertical—pointing straight up. As our jets slowed and it started to get really quiet, I stayed right in place. Both jets eventually fell backward when they ran out of airspeed.

As we started "flying" again with our noses pointed straight at the ground, I got right back in my spot. I didn't know if I had screwed up or not. Getting low on gas, we turned toward home, and the squadron commander did something unexpected. He tapped his head, pointed to me, and gave me the lead. I took it and drove us back to home base, wondering the whole time if I was in trouble. It was an odd flight, to say the least. After we got back, I eagerly awaited some feedback. I finally got three words: "Not too bad." I was ecstatic.

From that two-hour experience, I learned a ton about leadership.

Love and Appreciate Those You Serve

Sadly, the leadership model of appreciating those you serve is not well understood or widely deployed outside the military. Why is that? I feel the answer has a lot to do with how most people define and understand good leadership, coupled with the comparative consequences of poor leadership. Bad leadership in air warfare is unforgiving. Not surprisingly, I also feel that there is a paucity of true leadership in this country. Most people get the first and most important part completely wrong.

They don't think, *How I can serve and inspire those I lead?* Instead they think, *How can those I lead serve me?* In that flawed model, leadership becomes selfish and a morale killer. Why do so many people get this wrong? Wingmen, subordinates, or kids don't know exactly how to participate or contribute in a flawed model of leadership like this. True leadership is not about popularity and self-aggrandizement. Sometimes, being a servant-leader means doing things that are unpopular and challenging, but essential when managing risk or proceeding forward on a passion journey. Leaders and parents have to make tough choices that are often unpopular and require sacrifice. From how we allocate precious resources (time, talent, opportunity, compassion, grace, and treasure) to how we manage risk, despite trying to be equitable and fair to those we serve, tough choices are inevitable when resources are limited and priorities have to be made.

Leadership truly starts with a genuine love and appreciation for those you serve. It is interleaved with uncompromising loyalty to your superiors and your mission. I could go on and on about certain politicians falsely claiming leadership credentials, but I won't. I'd rather focus on the finer qualities you can instill in your children.

When We Fail

When I think of my leadership experiences spanning all situations and environments, there is one—a failure of sorts—that I always dwell on. We were returning from a very successful north Arabian Sea deployment on the USS *Constellation*. I was the carrier strike group operations officer and had the good fortune of working with one of the most gifted and virtuous leaders of all time, Vice Admiral Barry Costello.

To say the deployment had been arduous would be an understatement. We were the initial carrier strike group for Operation Iraqi

Freedom, and we were also the official night carrier in the north Arabian Sea during the first thirty days of operations. There were no easy days or nights. Every moment was full of challenges, high risk, high pressure, and high visibility. From bad weather to the threat of biological and chemical warfare, there were no sanctuaries. Through it all, Admiral Costello was strong, calm, decisive, and served his people exceptionally well. At the end of what seemed like years, our mission ended, and we were cleared to go home.

The timing of our return to San Diego couldn't have been better. Our success in Iraqi Freedom was now legendary, and it was soon to be July 4, 2003. We had some issues to deal with first, however. One of those issues involved a sailor on our staff who had gotten sick. Although we had a surgeon and medical staff on board no one could figure out exactly what was wrong with him. He continued to lose weight, and he looked terrible. We sent him to a hospital in Honolulu, our last port prior to heading home, but the doctors there could give no definitive diagnosis or recovery plan so they sent him back to the ship. Then, just before we pulled into San Diego, his conditioned worsened. We arranged for a medevac, and he was airlifted to the Navy hospital in San Diego, where he would ultimately undergo surgery for a digestive problem.

The rest of us refocused our attention on reunions with friends and families. It had been ten long months since we had been with them. The North Island carrier pier in San Diego was an amazing sight when we arrived. It was crowded with adoring loved ones wearing their most patriotic outfits of red, white, and blue. Everyone had a sign or banner declaring their love and pride for their precious sailor. We saw a clearly formed line comprised of those mothers who had given birth during our deployment. Tradition allows them to be the first to see their sailor and introduce their new child to his or her father. On the ship, a similar line was formed made up of the new dads. They were all dressed in pristine white, eagerly awaiting the opportunity to hold their baby for the first time. It was exciting, powerful, emotional stuff. There is no greater feeling in the world.

I finally spotted my "crew" out on the pier. What a beautiful sight: my wife, Terrie, and my three daughters, Sarah, Rachel, and Anna. My son wouldn't come along for a couple years. I finally got off the ship and reunited with them after what seemed an unusually long wait. We went home, got caught up on all the wonderful things that had happened in the past ten months, and simply enjoyed the blessing of being in each other's presence once again.

The next day I received a surprise phone call from our chief of staff. The admiral had asked him to call a meeting with all the department heads. *What could be wrong?* I thought. We had performed magnificently—there was no unfinished business. What could it be?

When we arrived for the meeting, the admiral promptly reminded us that we had violated the first rule of leadership. We had failed to serve our shipmate in the hospital. Not one of us had checked up on him. Not one of us had visited him. We had completely forgotten about a shipmate in need. He had no family nearby, so we were the only ones who should have cared enough to visit him. Soundly embarrassed, we quickly organized a staff visit plan to mitigate our failure.

"But we all knew that with leadership, you only get one chance to get it right."

The recovering sailor received our efforts graciously, and that helped somewhat to alleviate the guilt and embarrassment we all felt. But we all knew that with leadership, you only get one chance to get it right. Admiral Costello reminded us of what we already knew—leadership is first and foremost about service to others. We failed Costello, and we failed that sailor.

When We Don't Learn from Failure

I should have known better; I *did* know better. I had an issue a couple of years earlier that was clearly a preventable leadership failure. A young eighteen-year-old sailor had just joined our squadron. He was from the southeast United States and had a seventeen-year-old wife. He didn't earn very much money, so he couldn't afford a car. I started getting reports that he had been showing up perpetually late for work. When I asked about his status, I was told the problem was fixed.

In one of my daily squadron walk-arounds, I finally got to chat with him. My first impression was not good. His boots and pants were covered in mud. This was clearly not what I expected from my sailors. I pulled him aside and asked him why he was covered in mud. He told me it was because of the recent rain. When I pointed out that no one else was covered in mud, he explained that he walked through the fields to get to work rather than walking on the road because going by road took him 30 minutes longer.

"What? You walk to work?" I asked.

"Yes, sir," he replied.

As I continued to question him, I began to learn some surprising things that disturbed me. He and his wife were on a waiting list for base housing. They lived in an apartment in the local town ten miles from the squadron hangar where we worked. He initially used public transportation to get to work, but the bus dropped him off at the hangar five minutes late. When he started getting in trouble for being late, he decided that his only option was to walk the ten miles each day back and forth.

"If you take care of your people first, they will take care of you for life."

He had told no one of this dilemma up until this point. He had six levels of supervision below me, and not one of his supervisors knew the challenges this poor young man was facing. We could have helped him out with base housing; we could have allowed him to be a little late; or we could have paired him up with someone for a ride. Leadership had failed him. I failed him. He quickly went from "bad sailor" to "model sailor" in my book.

If you take care of your people first, they will take care of you for life. I immediately got him head-of-the-line privileges for base housing, and we activated a ride-share program during the transition. His appreciation and positive attitude were infectious. Although you may not see it all the time, children respond the same way to a parent who genuinely loves, serves, and sacrifices for those in their care.

One Bad Apple

In fighter squadrons, commanders change every eighteen months. And like any organization, some leaders are good and some are bad. The most critical part of this leadership renewal process is how quickly a bad CO can bring a great squadron down and how quickly a great CO can bring a bad squadron up. The shift is almost immediate, and it truly reflects how service-centric leaders can bring out the best in their subordinates. When everyone feels respected, valued, and a critical part of an important team where everyone is treated fairly, great things happen.

The Navy takes a dim view of commanders who can't hold that standard. Some accidently slip through the rigorous screening process, and some don't handle elevated pressure and challenge very well. When commanders are fired, the forensics show that they failed to learn the most important leadership lesson during their career: Leadership (and parenting) is all about service to others and knowing your personnel. And through that failure, they ended up creating what is known as a toxic command climate.

A year after my command tour, a renowned high-performing

F/A-18 squadron surprisingly experienced a series of silly embarrassing mishaps followed by an abrupt leadership change of their relatively new commander. For some reason, they had become plagued with serious accidents and many airborne emergencies. There were failed inspections, and they became recognized for substandard training-check rides. It didn't make sense. In a matter of months, the squadron that had been the best under the previous commander had become the worst, and they had become the laughingstock of the base. I knew many of the officers and chiefs in that squadron; they were some of the best professionals in the business. What could have possibly happened?

To put it bluntly, the new CO was a jerk. Aside from character and integrity issues, he had no respect for the people he served. He didn't trust them to do their jobs, and he micromanaged every facet of squadron business. His subordinates stopped caring and only performed out of fear of reprisal. They weren't allowed to be good wingmen. No investment was made in their growth or development. In such a toxic environment, it doesn't take very much time to produce spectacularly bad results. In naval aviation, this occasionally means mishaps, but it always means low morale, suboptimal performance, and wholesale misery. Fortunately, squadrons get a new CO every two years. In contrast, kids have parents for life, which makes it especially important for parents to get it right as soon as possible and endeavor to continuously improve.

Making Good Wingmen

How do you make good wingmen and good followers? It starts with service. And it starts with you.

continued

- Know your kids' attitudes and expectations. Think about swimming and how each kid eventually gets coaxed to go into deeper and deeper water.

- Know what they can do and how they add value. Place your kids in situations where they can be successful and feel like they are contributing.

- Share the big picture and show how important each person is. The big picture inspires kids and presents areas where their small contributions can make big impacts.

- Live up to your promises and show genuine concern and interest in their welfare and personal development. Use every opportunity to teach, show patience, and invest in their future.

Assuming you have no character, integrity, or courage issues, in time you will earn the respect of those you want to lead. With that respect, you will also gain loyalty, motivation, confidence, performance, and high morale. You will have wingmen you can count on.

Going for High Standards

Many leaders waste time, money, and talent by chasing irrelevant or nonproductive objectives. Instead of identifying and fixating on the key issue, they divert attention to symptoms and second-order consequences, leaving the key issue unresolved. Identifying and resolving key issues is an important part of leadership and parenting. Don't waste time, stress, and money chasing symptoms; resolve the key issue instead. Two of my kids went from exemplary to mediocre students seemingly overnight when they were in middle school. The key issue for each was different. For one it was social distractions, and for the other it was time management. My fighter pilot experience taught me to look beyond the obvious symptoms and keep digging until I found the key issue. By focusing on social boundaries and sanctuaries for one, and intrusive schedule management for the other, their grades started to recover.

At one point in my career I was in a squadron with some of the oldest F/A-18s. At that stage in their service life, several pilots applied the common wisdom that many of the aircraft were "bent," a term used when an airplane has been corrupted through age and use so that its stability is compromised. "Bent" also implied that the anomalies were unfixable and had to be accepted. Even so, we spent countless hours replacing flight control computers, motors, and surfaces. Nothing worked. We called in a systems expert who told us there was no such thing as a bent aircraft. He then asked what we'd been doing to our flight controls.

In the process of explaining what we'd done, we discovered our key issue. According to our maintenance manuals and common wisdom, we hadn't been doing anything wrong, per se. We just focused on the symptoms instead of going deeper to find and understand the key issue. If we had made the effort to go deeper rather than treat symptoms, we could have avoided wasting so much time, effort, and cost. It wasn't until we rejected common wisdom and focused on the key issue that we could move forward and make the proper adjustments. Then we flew perfectly.

As a leader, setting high but achievable standards predisposes your team toward key issue focus and resolution. A motivated, engaged, and loyal team with high standards will not only work hard—they will work smart. They become accustomed to challenging common wisdom and finding innovative ways to improve quality and speed. You get what you aim for, so to speak. All three of my older kids played college sports, and the only way they were able to be successful both athletically and academically was to set achievable goals and become disciplined about key issue management. That discipline started early in their development as we helped them connect their aspirations to actions associated with their key focus areas. And, as a fighter pilot parent, groupthink and common wisdom were always treated with suspicion.

"To some, it may seem hard, tough, and unpleasant being in an organization or family where leaders or parents set such high but achievable standards."

Setting high standards prevents laziness and sloppiness. If you want your kid to simultaneously excel at martial arts, lacrosse, and academics, as well as have time for video games, there is no room for wasted effort and energy. Setting high standards also forces everyone in the family to work together and be more efficient with family resources such as cars, drivers, and excess budget. With the manageable pressures created through pursuit of achievable and worthwhile goals, a system of efficiency, discipline, and prioritization emerges that will come in handy when the going gets tough. To some, it may seem hard, tough, and unpleasant being in an organization or family where leaders or parents set such high but achievable standards. That couldn't be further from the truth. Not only do these individuals stand out among their peers, they also enjoy extremely high morale, camaraderie, and FUN.

Grooming the Nuggets

In a war-fighting F/A-18 squadron, the biggest challenge we faced was continuous staff turnover. Every year we would lose 30 percent of our experienced pilots and technicians. After a deployment, it could easily climb to 50 percent. Squadrons that assimilate, train, and integrate new personnel the best generally had the most success, but it becomes a little more challenging when you have high pilot turnover, as was the case during my tour.

There are typically eighteen pilots in an F/A-18 squadron and twelve of those are on their very first operational tour. When these nuggets arrive, they have no qualifications and no experience other than basic jet training. On average, it takes about a year to make a nugget into a good wingman and another year to make them into a good flight lead. That typically leaves another year to earn the more advanced qualifications. Receiving three to four nuggets a year is challenging but manageable. Seven to eight is really hard. That's where we found ourselves.

The first instinct would be to slow it down, lower the standards, and ease them in. Our deployment schedule wouldn't allow that. Good leadership wouldn't allow that. We pressed ahead with the high standards required for combat success. We accelerated an already aggressive controlled failure training regimen and protected them with a very comprehensive risk-management program. They responded extremely well and were rewarded with accelerated flight qualifications.

When we arrived on station in the north Arabian Sea and started flying combat missions in Iraq, their performance was exceptional. When they had setbacks, they were minimal; they recovered quickly and kept on improving at an impressive rate. This wouldn't have happened had we lowered our standards. The nuggets would have struggled and would have become a combat liability. Whenever I'm tempted to lower standards, I immediately think back to that group of ordinary novice pilots and how they were able to quickly transform into pilots capable of extraordinary achievements. If you set a high bar for people, and support them along the way, they'll find a way to get there.

I took this approach when coaching new lacrosse players, including my son. Everything they did with their strong hand, I had them do with their weak hand, and I quickly increased the intensity and complexity as their skills improved. Not only did they progress at an amazing rate, but they also became self-motivated and passionate about the game—exactly like my squadron nuggets.

This special group of junior pilots quickly became battle-hardened combat veterans who went on to have impressive careers, which included Blue Angel and squadron command tours. During our time together, they were rewarded for their commitment to high standards with Battle Efficiency honors. The "Battle E" is awarded to the best F/A-18 squadron in the Navy, and these pilots earned it. My little lacrosse players had similar success stories.

When Standards Are Lowered for the Few

When I served in the Navy, political pressure associated with the lack of gender and ethnic diversity among pilots in operational jet squadrons insidiously led to lower standards. The all-volunteer force was a frequent target of forced political correctness and social engineering—despite the realities of combat readiness and safety impacts. On the heels of the infamous Tailhook scandal[3] and the sexual harassment controversy that followed, the Navy was in desperate need of an image improvement. In addition to destroying the careers of many undeserving leaders, the

---

3 The Tailhook scandal involved 100 United States Navy and U.S. Marine Corps aviation officers who were alleged to have sexually assaulted or engaged in otherwise "improper and indecent" conduct at a conference in 1991 in Las Vegas, Nevada.

Navy also decided that they would be first to place women in combat strike-fighter aircraft.

In order to rapidly produce combat-ready female pilots and aircrew, the Navy couldn't wait the three years it normally takes to screen, train, and nurture a typical candidate. They looked at what they already had in the wings. Women had been flying Navy jets for quite some time, but mostly in support roles. That group seemed like a great pool of women to lead the charge. It could've been—but it wasn't.

Up until that point, these women had been brought up to be support pilots, not fighter pilots. They weren't required to know how to land on a ship day or night, and they had no tactical training experience. What they routinely did was tow targets, fly simple profiles for ship training and services, and clear ranges in advance of missile practice shoots. They were nowhere close to being carrier strike fighter pilots. And because they were allowed to skip the normal training progression, they also skipped the filters everyone else had to go through to earn their membership in a very high-risk enterprise. When that deficiency was combined with years of simple, unsophisticated, shore-based operations, the women pilots were set up for failure. It didn't matter; the Navy was going to be first.

Advancing Before You Are Ready

One of those pilots was a former student of mine, Kara Hultgreen. She became the very first Navy female fighter pilot. On a beautiful October day in 1994, while attempting to land her F-14A Tomcat on board the USS *Abraham Lincoln*, she lost control of her jet, failed to eject, and died when the aircraft crashed into the water alongside the ship. The official report attributed the crash to a critical engine malfunction, a

continued

faulty landing approach, and failure to eject in time. The horrendous crash video is available in perpetuity on YouTube.

When I knew Kara, she was a very capable student aviator. She was serious, motivated, and performed on par with her male counterparts. She was always prepared and had no problems completing her required flights. If she had gone on to F-14A training right after getting her wings, she may well have been successful. Unfortunately, that option wasn't available to her—or any female—at that time. Instead, she went on to fly EA-6A Prowlers in Key West, Florida, for three years.

I can't think of two more dissimilar airplanes or missions. The EA-6A provided electronic threat simulations for ships during their pre-deployment training phase. They carried wing-mounted pods specifically designed to emulate threat radar systems. The F-14A, in contrast, was a high-performance, high-speed interceptor, designed to find and engage enemy aircraft, as well as drop bombs. The EA-6A flew simple scripted maneuvers, while the F-14A flew very dynamic, high-"g," rapidly changing missions. Kara's EA-6A squadron was land-based. Her F-14A squadron was ship-based. The EA-6A usually operated alone. The F-14A usually operated in groups of four or more aircraft.

So, for three years Kara developed habit patterns, routines, and muscle memory that were completely useless to her when transitioning to the F-14A. The pace, complexity, and challenge were polar opposites. More insidious, however, was the added challenge of also having to unlearn all the things she had been doing in the EA-6A. Habits are a stubborn thing. Having flown multiple jets throughout my career, I know from experience that unlearning habits is not an easy task, especially when going from the simple to the complex. It can even be challenging to fly the same type aircraft but with different software loads.

In extreme situations, though, it is those stubborn habit patterns that immediately step forward and try to save the day for you. Bad habits bring bad results. Whenever I see people trying to shortcut the delicate process required for skill mastery, I immediately think of Kara and that initial cadre of women aviators. Political correctness got the best of them. Although a great idea, and way overdue, it was horribly led and executed.

As the father of three girls, I want my daughters to have every opportunity that a man has, but I also want them to deserve it and earn it. Otherwise it is meaningless. And in the world of strike fighters, it is downright dangerous.

As a strike fighter squadron commander, I wanted competent and proficient pilots of high integrity and character in my ranks. I didn't care if they were gay, white, black, men, or women. There are no shortcuts in this business. Frauds quickly stand out. The women who would eventually graduate through the normal process became standout pilots and officers. Many of the original group of women pilots who were rushed through had difficulties.

"There are no shortcuts in this business."

As the Navy moved forward, it became obvious that there were problems. Many women had significant setbacks while completing their training phases. If it had been a man instead of a woman, they would have been terminated from training—plain and simple. But with cover from the top and powerful advocacy, they were not allowed to fail. Instead, their performance standards were lowered—shamelessly.

Not surprisingly, when they eventually got to the fleet, they weren't ready for what awaited them, and therefore they were inherently dangerous. It wasn't their fault either. Ironically, in the Navy's eagerness to place women in fighter jets, they ended up creating a set of conditions that would ultimately place them further back. By advancing them before they were ready, these early women pioneers failed to earn the respect of their male counterparts and suffered significant performance issues when they arrived in the fleet. They were set up to fail.

It never pays to hold different people to different standards. It creates resentment and morale issues. It undermines every tenet of proven leadership. Thankfully, as women continued to go through the optimal training pipeline—renowned for high standards and fair assessment—they eventually overcame and reversed the initial stigma on female pilots created by ignoring the time-honored controlled failure process. I have flown with some of the most talented fighter pilots on the planet; many are women. The country is blessed for their service.

Actions, Not Words

Parenting and leadership are not about popularity, public opinion, or picking favorites. They are about fair treatment and making tough and timely decisions. Actions, not words, determine your authenticity. You have to be genuine or you will be easily called out, and your position and motivation will always be placed under suspicion. These are the important things for leaders to get right, and it is equally important for parents to get them right too. You typically only get one chance, so you have to examine the potential perceptions of everything you say and do. As a parent, it is extremely important to avoid the do-what-I-say, not-what-I-do scenarios. Unless it concerns a strictly adult concept, you lose credibility every time you don't follow your own rules. My wife and I often cite our whereabouts (or buddy system) rule. Before we could track each other on mobile phones, we religiously let each other know where we were and when we were leaving. Not only does it give people who care about you peace of mind, but it also lets them know when to expect your return in case you run into trouble.

Along do-what-I-say, not-what-I-do lines, when I think of the absolute worst leaders I've encountered, it is the excuse makers and bullies that I reserve my greatest disdain for. You know them—mistakes are never their fault. They always find someone else to blame, and it's usually the most junior and most inexperienced people around them that get blamed for their mistakes. I have a story to illustrate what I mean.

In early 1991, I needed to refresh my carrier qualifications before I could join an air wing already deployed to the north Arabian Sea in support of Operation Desert Storm. Our training carrier was the USS *Theodore Roosevelt*, and we would stage out of Oceana, Virginia. A hurricane had just swept across the East Coast, and the weather was still unsettled and volatile.

" . . . (Y)ou lose credibility every time you don't follow your own rules."

I was the flight lead for the first group of four airplanes to fly out to the ship. I had with me two nugget pilots and a senior officer who was transitioning from A-7 Corsair IIs to F/A-18s. I briefed them on the flight and went through the entire carrier landing and catapult procedures. I also went through all the emergency procedures and contingencies. Then I spent some time discussing a very important and critical difference between the A-7 and the F/A-18 during catapult.

In the F/A-18, one of most unusual and counterintuitive things a pilot does during catapult is to take his hand off the controls and grab a handhold (the "towel rack") on the right of the cockpit just below the canopy. As the jet leaves the ship, the pilot then lowers his hand behind the stick and starts flying the jet away from the water when it is airborne. For A-7 pilots, this was very uncomfortable because in an A-7, pilots would launch with their hand cupped behind the stick and keep it there throughout the launch. If they accidentally grabbed the stick on the F/A-18, they ran the risk of inducing exaggerated flight control movements prior to

getting airborne—which usually translated into unacceptable nose por-
poising and an immediate descent off the catapult.

After we launched, we immediately started dodging thunderstorms
en route to the ship. The post–hurricane winds were still very strong, so
I wasn't surprised when we checked in with ship air operations and discovered that the current landing winds were forty-five to fifty knots—
way too high for training. They decided to bring us down in between
wind gusts and wait until the winds stabilized within training limits.

We all landed uneventfully. The senior officer was parked forward
just behind the catapults. The rest of us were parked alongside the
landing area in the middle of the ship. We had a great view of aircraft
approaching and landing, and we could even watch them take off without any obstruction! They chained us down and connected fuel hoses as
we waited for the winds to die down.

After about thirty minutes I noticed activity up forward. They
removed the chains and chocks from the senior officer's jet and spotted
him on catapult two. I was anxious to get going, so I was a little disappointed when I seemed to be ignored. Then another jet was moved
behind the other catapult. There was still no interest in moving me.
My two nugget wingmen looked at me for guidance, and I shrugged
my shoulders and transmitted again that we were ready to go. I felt
the vibration of the aircraft on catapult two as it went to full power. I
turned my head just in time to see the senior pilot launch.

The jet went off the ship very flat and dipped just a little before I
saw an explosion and then something separate from the fuselage. The
pilot had ejected, as became obvious when his parachute bloomed. He
began a nice, easy descent along the left side of the ship, entering the
water right in front of where I was sitting. At least he was OK. But what
about the aircraft?

It was still flying.

During the ejection, it had already begun climbing, and it continued climbing until it reached about 2,000 feet. For a moment, I considered that maybe it was a two-seat F/A-18, and there was a pilot still inside, but I knew there weren't any two-seat jets out there. That jet was literally flying itself. At 2,000 feet, it started a level left turn just as though it was setting up to land. Then it started another left turn at less than a mile from the ship heading in the opposite direction, still at an altitude of 2,000 feet.

Then I got nervous.

Suddenly this unmanned jet turned again, lowered its nose, and took a direct path right toward my two wingmen and me. We had nowhere to go. They looked over at me for advice, and again I shrugged. The only thing I could think to do was to lower my seat. I knew it wouldn't do any good, but it sure made me feel better at the time. My wingmen followed suit while my eyes remained glued to that unpiloted jet.

Still on a direct path, and getting bigger in my eyes as the distance between us quickly diminished, the jet flinched ever so slightly and rolled just enough to avoid hitting the ship—and us—but now it was tracking for the pilot still in the water. Thankfully it rolled one more time, just narrowly missing the floating pilot. It was so close to the ship when it crashed into the water that large pieces of the wreckage rained down on the flight deck, sending everyone running for cover. Other than some scraped flight deck crew hands as they dove out of the way of falling debris, no one was injured. What a blessing!

We immediately shut down our engines and went inside the ship. After receiving notification that the pilot was OK, I went to watch the launch tapes. Based on the exaggerated flight control movements during the catapult, it became clear to all of us that the senior officer grabbed the controls during launch. It probably spooked him when he initially porpoised and started descending, at which time he obviously panicked and decided to eject. It was his first launch in a new airplane in a critical flight regime—in other words, a phase of flight where a pilot must perform perfectly since the margin of error is so slim. Based on what the airplane did after he ejected, it was also clear that there were no mechanical problems with the jet; it flew great. Pilot error. Case closed.

"Making mistakes and underperforming is embarrassing but certainly human. People understand, forgive, and respect you when you own up to your mistakes."

"Not so fast," said the senior officer. He was quick to offer a couple of excuses. He claimed there was an engine problem during catapult, and he was also adamant that he never touched the stick. What really hurt, though, was his claim that I never briefed him on any of the catapult procedures before we launched. (Of course, that wouldn't really have mattered if he had never touched the stick.) By throwing everyone else under the bus, he proved to me he was unfit to lead. He was eventually removed from his flying position as a squadron commander, and I'm pretty sure he never flew again.

Own Up

Leaders and parents both must have the courage to own up to what they and their subordinates and kids do and take the heat that follows as a result. Making mistakes and underperforming is embarrassing but certainly human. People understand, forgive, and respect you when you own up to your mistakes. When you blame others and make excuses, you really fool no one, and you completely undermine your entire leadership and parenting foundation. My wife and I tell on ourselves immediately to try and set the example with our kids: "I forgot to do this . . . I accidentally backed into the car . . . I made the mess . . . but I'll clean it up."

The Blue Angels and Leadership

The Blue Angels probably provide the most visible example of the important leadership quality of owning up. The commander, known as the air boss, is the most important safety factor on the team. If he misjudges or misses his cues, he runs the risk of not only crashing his jet but crashing all the other jets on the team. A few past air bosses have come to terms with their inability to consistently provide that critical safety buffer and have resigned for the good of the team. I respect that. That's what good leaders do.

The Glory Belongs to the Team

I have never seen a good leader comfortably accept praise for a team accomplishment. The praise and acknowledgment rightly belongs to the group and their individual contributions. Good leaders humbly redirect recognition away from themselves and toward the key team members who were directly responsible for the success. The glory belongs to them. This is nonnegotiable.

Conversely, when someone on your team fails, good leaders shoulder the responsibility for the failure, as long as it's not the result of

"When one of us fail, we all fail, and we as parents must take ownership and harvest the key lessons to prevent future failure."

an individual character flaw or integrity failure. You can never be held accountable for someone else's character and integrity indiscretions. Families are teams, too, just like military teams. When one of us in the family fails, we all fail, and we as parents must take ownership and harvest the key lessons to prevent future failure.

The good leader or parent endeavors to understand why a failure occurred and take the steps necessary to prevent it from happening in the future. By diffusing the guilt and remorse that a subordinate or kid feels after letting the team or family down, you signal your commitment to continuous improvement and your exclusive nondelegable accountability for any bad things that happen. Taking ownership really resonates with kids, and they are often motivated to preclude you from ever being in that awkward position again. Families that push hard will have failures from time to time as they chase perfection. Be there for your team.

These concepts may be easy to understand, but they are much harder to put into practice. Once again, it usually comes down to courage. While this may not be obvious, one of the key leadership qualities that demands the most courage to demonstrate is delegation. It is tough to simply give away or share control when there is the possibility of risk and failure. Good leaders and good parents recognize the value of decisions that are delegated at the appropriate level. Correct delegation improves speed of action and places a premium on child competency. It develops leadership attributes in others more quickly and greatly improves morale. Have the courage to delegate.

I tell my own kids and the young kids I coach: "Take control of your own lives. Know where you are supposed to be and at what time. Verify that you have everything you need before you leave. And whatever you are doing, bring your best effort, energy, and focus—or it isn't worth doing in the first place."

★★★

 # FIGHTER PILOT PARENT TAKEAWAYS— Leadership and Service

★ Good leadership is good parenting, and both are all about service to others and knowing your personnel.

★ Good leaders and good parents take care of their people by being calm, predictable, and responsive to their team's needs.

★ Good leaders and good parents don't micromanage; rather, they create situations where their people can be successful.

★ Good leaders and good parents are constantly training their replacements or teaching their kids to lead themselves. Don't be afraid to delegate.

★ Good leaders and good parents constantly challenge others to exceed their own perceived capabilities and make a constant investment in building self-confidence.

★ Good leaders and good parents are uncompromising when it comes to character, integrity, and courage. Kids raised this way tend to be successful in life.

CHAPTER FIVE

LIKABILITY, HUMILITY, GRACE, AND HUMOR

———

Just as I was about to take over an F/A-18 squadron, a very wise mentor of mine told me that the most important thing I must do as a commanding officer is to be likeable. Forget about the flying stuff, he said. When I think about his advice, I immediately think about the sports stars everyone loves—Peyton Manning, Tim Tebow, Tim Duncan, David Robinson. They're surprisingly likeable, humble, and grounded, despite their unbelievable talent and success. How did they get that way? Why doesn't everyone emulate them?

I believe that likability and being grounded both stem from a strong appreciation of self-deprecating humor, humility, and grace. And if you can project all three qualities simultaneously, you're going to be likeable. It's really quite easy. When you make people feel better about themselves, they like you. When people perceive that you are genuinely interested in them and what they have to say, human nature dictates that they will like you. By simply focusing on others, listening to them, and placing their interests ahead of yours, they will like you.

Have you ever heard someone say, "I don't care if anyone likes me"? This is nonsense. Everyone wants to be liked. So what prevents people from becoming likeable, humble, and grounded? I would argue it is lack of humility. People like to think they're better, smarter, more experienced, cooler, wealthier, and everything else than those around them. Being humbled is painful and awkward. It means that you've failed something or someone. However, deliberately revisiting humbling moments is important in order to extract learning value from them.

Another stumbling block to achieving humility is scalability. The more successful you become, the more you cheat death, the more you separate yourself from everyone else, the greater number of humility reserves you will need to stay grounded.

Many people might assume that being a fighter pilot is especially dangerous territory if one's aim is to preserve humility. Blockbuster movies seem to assert this theme whenever they can; think *Top Gun* and Tom Cruise. A clear threat to humility definitely exists when a pilot survives a rigorous training gauntlet, masters challenging skills, and ultimately enjoys the unique privilege of being able to "kiss the sky" or "touch the face of God" each and every day in his or her job. But this phenomenon is not isolated to fighter pilots. Anyone who achieves some level of success has a tendency to forget how they achieved that success. Their sacrifice, their perseverance, their mentors, and their good fortune are often devalued, and consequently their humility suffers. They forget where they came from and how they got where they are. People who are expected to perform flawlessly every time—independent of complexity or scope—also have interesting humility challenges.

At one point, I was the patient of a surgeon whose specialty was hands and fingers. After several visits where we shared our backgrounds and career challenges (after all the medical stuff was out of the way), we developed a comfort level with each other that allowed him to talk about his personal life. During one of my last office visits, he broke down and shared the pain he was suffering from a failing marriage.

I believe he thought that because of my profession, I was one of the few people who could understand the pressure he was under. As a surgeon, his patients expected perfect execution 100 percent of the time. An occasional mangled hand would not be tolerated very well.

As good as he was, he was finally faced with the reality that perfection was impossible. He had ultimately sacrificed humility in support of his illusion of perfection. This paradox pressurized his work life because he set extraordinary performance standards for himself. Because of the additional intense pressure at work, other parts of his personal life suffered, and his marriage was falling apart as a result. When we have humility, we have a great defense against expectation creep and the pressure to perform that comes with it. Humility provides a realistic perspective and a healthy comfort with imperfection. It allows you to recognize your limitations and seek the additional support you may need, or defer to others that are more capable.

> "Humility provides a realistic perspective and a healthy comfort with imperfection."

This type of pressure among fighter pilots creates a similar type of humility challenge. For many elite performers in high-risk professions, the tendency to self-identify as a super human is a common theme and can be very dangerous. Considering yourself a super human doesn't leave much room for humility. Navy fighter pilots have a unique way of managing that threat, as you will see in the following.

When You're a Nobody

I was born with the name Charles Bradford Conners. I grew up as Brad to my family and friends. When I joined my first Navy squadron, I was christened "Brick" as part of a long and successful tradition of providing what I call humility insurance. I continue to use that name to this day as a reminder of where I started. At the time, I was blessed with abundant humility. I had only twenty-eight carrier arrestments, no deployments, and no combat time. I was a nobody, a new guy, a nugget. But the new culture in which I found myself was not going to let that condition last very long.

The "new guy call sign" process (coming up with pseudo names to be used for tactical communication) was the first of many humility enhancers I was to experience. Not only was it fun for the rest of the squadron, but it was also an essential rite of passage and a significant, career-long humility tool for me. The key to the process was to confer a call sign on someone that would link them forever to an embarrassing point of origin. Unfortunately, the importance and utility of this process is often missed by the public and media as a direct result of some infrequent abuse on the part of a limited number of squadrons as well as the misperceptions created by popular movies.

During the post-Tailhook era, this process was placed on hold indefinitely. Then it got worse. When pilots were issued orders to their first fleet squadron, the set of orders included an official call sign that was to be used. As you may have guessed, it was promptly ignored by everyone. Eventually this absurd naming protocol was terminated. We had lots of fun with it, though. We all imagined an elite team of call sign writers at the Pentagon thinking up new names for each pilot. Some of the names they came up with were hilarious, and some even stuck.

In my day, and in my squadron, the process was fairly well standardized. A new pilot would walk into the squadron ready room and immediately find a white board full of potential call signs. There could literally be hundreds of them. Some were variations of the pilot's name. When that well ran dry, the names focused on the pilot's hometown or alma mater. And toward the end of the list, random, absurd names ruled. For the new pilot, despite what you may think, this was all a dream come true—not a hazing ritual. It meant he had arrived.

From the hundreds of proposed names, the squadron would quickly vote on the best, and that name would become a temporary call sign. That's right: temporary. The final name wouldn't come for a while. My first-round name was "Darby"—my real name backwards with a "y" at the end (not very imaginative). The final name could take several weeks—or even months—of nervously waiting for an embarrassing event to present itself and thereby give birth to the new "perfect" name.

The committee who had named me consisted of great aviators and officers with interesting call signs such as Shrubs, Hook, Badrod, Muddy, Grover, Hoss, Bilbo, JR, TL, Curly Joe, Nanny, Psycho, and Notso, and they were ready to pounce. In my case, it would take about three months.

We were scheduled to join the entire air wing in Fallon, Nevada, for training. During this four-week training phase, we would practice complex tactics against sophisticated missile and air threats. We would build the complexity over time, leading up to complex strike tactics with very large groups of aircraft toward the end. It was not uncommon to have forty-plus aircraft in a single training strike opposed by fifteen to twenty adversary or "red" aircraft. This was the Cold War, for heaven's sake. As you can imagine, everything was new, exciting, and challenging for me.

A friend and peer who was in another air wing had been practicing the same things a few months earlier—but with bad results. He and his flight lead had been flying through the mountains, at low altitude, when low clouds boxed them in. Fearing impact with a cloud-covered mountaintop, the lead abruptly pulled up, leaving my friend behind, nose pointing up, away from the ground and in the clouds. As the jet ran out of airspeed, stalled, and then fell back to the ground like a chunk of concrete, my friend ejected. Although the ejection was successful, he floated down through the clouds and ended up landing in snow up to his neck. He couldn't move. A rescue helicopter eventually picked him up, but I couldn't get that vision out of my head each time I went flying—and it was summer by then. I didn't want to be "that guy."

Brick Pickle

I hadn't received my final call sign yet, and we were approaching the end of training. I was feeling pretty good about how things were going, and I was gaining the respect of my squadron mates. I felt fortunate to be scheduled for one of the most challenging missions yet. I was going to be on the executive officer's (XO's) wing. I had better not screw up!

My executive officer (XO) and I were part of a fifty-plane attacking package that would transit south to conduct our mission in a large Air Force training area near the famous and secretive Area 51. Rumor had it there would be twenty to twenty-five planes opposing us. My mission was to ingress at low altitude, 200 feet, with four 500-pound bombs configured with a special tail fin used for low-altitude attacks called snake-eye fins. The fins would pop out and slow the bomb down when released, allowing us to drop at very low altitudes and high speed without risk of blowing up the pilot. Our targets were part of a simulated airfield complex. As we descended and pushed on our ingress route, the radios were busy with high anxiety chatter.

There were nonstop transmissions describing threat activity, simulated air-to-air weapons exchanges, kill calls that removed the simulated dead aircraft from the exercise, and lots of other stuff. I couldn't process any of it, so I just focused on my little happy world at 200 feet flying through canyons and over desert. The one thing I remembered from the brief—because it was stressed so often and was a frequent debrief point on other missions—was to make sure to select all the proper switches so when the "pickle" button (the little red weapons-release button on top of the stick) was hit, the bombs would come off.

We pressed on. The magic distance from the target to finalize the switch positions was determined to be ten miles. Not eleven or nine, but ten. At exactly ten miles from the target, I took great pride in selecting the last and final switch, known as the master arm toggle switch, that would allow my weapons to come off and blow up, thus finalizing my checklist. When I hit that red pickle button, bombs were definitely going to come off and explode.

At five miles, I started looking for my target and elevated my jet a little. Thinking back, although it was a training exercise, it was very similar to combat, and when carrying real bombs, risks are always amplified. While scanning for my specific ground target, I noticed two blurs go between my XO and me. I immediately heard my flight lead tell me to break right, a defensive term used to counter an imminent attack by aggressively turning—in this case to the right. The "bad" guys had definitely found us. I blindly followed my lead's instructions. I quickly spotted the two adversary A-4 Skyhawks and saw them turning back toward us. Although they couldn't carry or shoot real missiles at us in training, we honored their offensive position as if they could. In order to keep sight of them, I switched my hand on the control stick from my right hand to my left. I wanted to use my right hand to position my body better in order to look over my right shoulder and maintain eye contact with the bad guys. As soon as I did this, I felt the airplane shudder and rock from side to side. Uh-oh, did my bombs just come off? Yup.

Thankfully, because of my altitude and maneuvers, the bombs never armed and therefore never exploded. It would have been bad if they had. The area where they landed was in the closed portion of the training range, where Air Force ordnance disposal technicians were visually searching for unexploded ordnance and making them safe when discovered. Now they had four more to deal with, thanks to me. The Air Force was not happy. I was immediately and completely dejected, and I thought I would never fly again. And if I did fly, I suspected I would have a new call sign by tomorrow. It wouldn't take them very long.

After I landed, I went straight to the ready room and shared my side of the story with squadron and air wing leadership. Hmm . . . they didn't seem too mad or overly concerned. Maybe I'd keep my wings after all. In the background, I heard several of the naming committee muttering "Brick Pickle." It was soon to be official. Before the day ended, "Pickle" was dropped, and I was forever to be known as "Brick." My squadron mates commiserated with me and shared their early new-guy mistakes—but none were quite as bad as mine, or so it seemed to me. At least I didn't shoot anyone down, and they were adamant that I join them at the Officers' Club where the air wing would typically congregate after flight operations were over for the day. It was the last thing I wanted to do, but I went anyhow, with my tail firmly tucked between my legs.

The Meaning of Grace

As the evening passed, I thought I was blending into the background sufficiently. Then, one by one, every fighter squadron commander, the air wing commander, and several senior aviators found me and pulled me aside. These guys were my heroes. These guys were great leaders. What each and every one of them did for me in that loud, raucous bar changed my life, and it made me love naval aviation more than I already did.

It started with the air wing commander, a former Blue Angel air boss. Every encounter following the one with him was pretty similar. It would start with some friendly ribbing, followed by some standard derogatory joking about the Air Force, our sister service. Then there would be an all-kidding-aside serious moment when they would reassure me that everything would be OK, and everyone would wrap up with their true confession story, all seemingly much worse than my significant transgression. There were crash stories, running out of gas stories, and bombing wrong target stories—even a landing with the landing gear up story. Whether they knew it or not, each one of these encounters was a selfless act of love and mercy that I clearly didn't deserve. There is a word for what they were doing. I learned it in church: grace.

> "From those leaders' examples, I learned that when you correct someone, do so without anger or revenge, and with your aim being to improve that person."

From those leaders' examples, I learned that when you correct someone, do so without anger or revenge, and with your aim being to improve that person. Maybe if I had been more experienced, that same grace wouldn't have been extended to me. But fortunately, it had been, and it was very powerful. From that point on, I knew I would do anything I could to earn back and redistribute the same grace that was offered to me.

When someone is trying hard but an honest mistake is made, grace can be an essential leadership and parenting tool. I do make exceptions, though. It's a different story when an act is purposeful or directly related to a character or integrity flaw. I hold a tight grip on grace under those conditions. I also withhold grace when extending grace would negatively impact morale or add unacceptable risk. I've had to do this a number of times when it became clear that a pilot was a danger to himself and others. Grace, under those circumstances, meant helping them find a new profession. I've had similar situations with my kids where I had to either address repeat behavior compromises or the rare and total disregard for personal safety, as I experienced with my daughter and her covert mission to Van Nuys in my Jeep.

Humility and grace go hand in hand. They both raise the likability scale substantially. Likability is especially important when you are trying to teach. In the multiple elite training institutions I've been a part of, likability was the most important factor we considered when we were hiring staff. A likeable instructor is approachable, trusted, and sought after for extra help and assistance. Students learn faster, retain information longer, and perform better when they are paired with likeable instructors. With children, it is especially important to always be accessible and patient, but as any parent knows, it is easy to be distracted. That's why I frequently remind myself to be careful to avoid being distracted when my children ask for help with schoolwork or other challenges. I want them to always feel comfortable using me as their first and favorite resource for help. I don't always get this right, but I've made it a focus area for improvement.

Looking for Likeable

Ten years after my call sign christening, I became an instructor responsible for the very same air wing training syllabus at the newly created Naval Strike and Air Warfare Center (now called the Naval Aviation Warfighting Development Center) in Fallon, Nevada—also the then-new home of Top Gun. My new Top Gun CO was the very same CO involved in the ball bearing incident I mentioned in Chapter Three. The instructors, all hand-selected, were the Navy's experts on tactics, threats, and weapon systems. As you might expect, they were especially intimidating from the junior aircrew's perspective. Even worse was the fact that the older and more experienced aircrews were extremely judicious when conferring respect toward junior instructor aviators and were typically of the opinion that they couldn't learn anything from us junior instructors. So, for this very special group of senior instructors, and for the viability of the training program we were responsible for, we had to find ways to be even more likeable.

We not only had to overcome the intimidation barrier, we also had to earn the respect of our most important customers—those leaders who would be responsible for leading men and women in air combat. We used a number of different methods with limited success. Our CO even issued us copies of his three favorite likeability books. Everyone read the first one, *Leadership Secrets of Attila the Hun*. No surprise there. Most instructors read the second book, *The One Minute Manager*, because it was short. No one read the final book, *How to Win Friends & Influence People*, probably because it was perceived as being long and not invoking the same sort of warrior-like qualities as say, *Leadership Secrets of Attila the Hun*.

How to Get to Likeable

○ **Set the Rules**.

With all those copies of likability books sitting around, and the last of the three unread, we decided to put some rules in place that would

continued

make people want to read *How to Win Friends & Influence People*—and thereby (we hoped) increase likability.

✪ **Work Together.**

We worked in close proximity to each other and as part of teams when we trained air wings. If anybody was rude, curt, disagreeable, insulting, condescending, or sarcastic to an aviator in a complex training or a real-life combat environment, either in person or on the phone, someone would know.

✪ **Be Accountable.**

Working together so closely, we could also hold each other accountable. We had many other behavior incentive policies that usually were punishable by fine, but this one was different.

✪ **Set the Punishment.**

It was simple: If anyone witnessed a likability or humility violation by an instructor, they could immediately assign a form of reading punishment—in any reasonable amount—from *How to Win Friends & Influence People*. (It's actually a great book with wonderful advice, so this punishment was somewhat of a gimmick to get people to read it.)

The first violation didn't take long to happen. An instructor was heard to say, "That's a stupid idea." As a first offense, only one page of reading was assigned as punishment. But then instructors started having fun with it. In short order, they were going out of their way to find violators and assign punishment. We had to update the policy in order to add much greater detail with respect to violation criteria and standard punishment. Contested charges usually came to me for reconciliation. Repeat offenders, who typically weren't aware of the moment they crossed the line, started reading the book to avoid reading the book. It was amazing.

> ○ **Make a Team.**
>
> Within weeks, violations tapered off, and it would be fair to say that by that stage, everyone had either read the book as punishment, read it to avoid punishment, or read it because they got interested in it. Whatever the reason, our aircrew in training experienced us in a much different way. We seemed more likeable, humble, and approachable. When the trainees left and eventually deployed, they routinely came back to us for assistance if they experienced any unique problems or wanted to share lessons learned. We had earned their respect, and they felt as though they were part of our team. Sometimes it's just that easy.

Healthy Humility

Humility plays a key role in confidence management. In any endeavor, especially one involving high risk and complexity, both overconfidence and low confidence can be equally dangerous.

With low confidence, people tend to be tentative, indecisive, and nonaggressive. In a fast-paced environment, they fail to take advantage of limited opportunities that may present themselves. Late or slow decisions plague those who lack confidence—which usually translates to mission- or performance-failure. As we've learned, a controlled failure training environment builds confidence and high first-time success simultaneously. As a parent and coach, I find that low confidence is not uncommon in new situations, and I devote quite a bit of time convincing those who suffer from low confidence that they have what it takes by reminding them of their successes and accomplishments or comparing their journey with those who have gone before them.

But overconfidence can be far worse. With this condition, pilots tend to overestimate their own skill, underestimate the enemy's, make impetuous decisions, wing it, and accept excessive risk. It follows that they are too aggressive, they frequently change their mind, and they are unpredictable. Occasionally, these tendencies become so bad that there is no apparent fear of death. As you can imagine, any organization would not be well served with excessive risk takers like these, especially in naval aviation. Of the pilots I've known that meet this profile, many have died. With kids, balancing this side of the confidence spectrum can often be resolved through recalibrating their version of reality and encouraging them to think through all the possible obstacles they can and can't control. Sometimes, however, experience may be the only thing that will work.

A good scare usually brings these overly confident people back to earth, but at times other methods of humility and confidence-calibration are necessary. Normally, I would never support using targeted humor that threatens another person's pride, peace of mind, or professionalism, but for these cases, exceptions are warranted. Poking fun at someone who has overstepped their legitimate humility and confidence boundary is therapeutic for individuals and those around them. I've ventured into overconfidence territory occasionally myself, usually without knowing it, and it has always been humor that gets me right again with the people that mean the most to me. In aviation, humor-based overconfidence corrections usually happen during flight debriefs where you pick yourself apart before anyone else gets to. When coaching kids, I talk about the things I could have or should have done better during practice or games. And at home, we are merciless with each other.

"... (T)he best families and military units I've seen take pride in their openness—and their ability to give each other important, unbiased, yet tactful feedback."

In close squadrons and in close families,

it is rare that anyone gets a free pass when egos or confidence get too big. In fact, the best families and military units I've seen take pride in their openness—and their ability to give each other important, unbiased, yet tactful feedback. Typically, it's not the inexperienced or junior members you have to worry about so much; it's the more senior, more "salty" ones, like Mom and Dad. When humor is applied as a humility and overconfidence tool, not only do you get to rebalance both, you also receive the benefit of a significant boost in group morale. There is a special unifying quality when it comes to bringing the big dogs down a notch. Humor is by far the best vehicle to accomplish the objectives of improving humility and curbing overconfident egos.

Taming the Biggest Egos

How does taming big egos work in a Navy fighter squadron? Just like in life. It doesn't take too long to figure out who has the biggest egos, and once those people have been identified, they immediately become the focus of every junior pilot. Every habit, every mannerism, everything they say or do is scrutinized. Imitations are rehearsed and perfected. Every mistake they make is catalogued. Then the junior pilots sit and wait for the right opportunity to pounce.

During deployments, the best squadrons employ a regular method for humor-based ego, humility, and confidence checks. Over the course of a fly day, whether combat operations or not, any action or inaction that hints of excessive ego or that publicly embarrasses the squadron can be nominated for a daily "award." Anything from inappropriate radio transmissions to highly visible procedural violations during flight operations around the ship are fair game.

Automatic nominations occur when the captain of the ship, the air boss, the air group commander, or the admiral ask to personally see the offender. On any given day, there may be three or more total nominations. When flight operations are over for the day, the junior officers get to present their findings, and the entire squadron votes. The presenter is obligated to present in a humorous but respectful fashion. The winner, aside from the public humility check he receives, gets the honor of wearing a special name tag for twenty-four hours until the next session of voting.

The best part is that the winner is rarely the newer, inexperienced pilot. It is most often the pilot with a growing ego, too much confidence, or a humility problem. And those who can't laugh at themselves soon discover that the search for future violations refocuses on them, or they become the main subject for skit material at frequent deployment awards and recognition ceremonies. Entertainment is always expected. It is like a delicate ecosystem where egos, humility, and confidence are all kept in balance.

Through this process, everyone learns a valuable lesson: Humor is used to modify certain behaviors without alienating anyone, and with it, overall team performance and professionalism is enhanced. I can't imagine how anybody can work or operate in a high-stress, boring, or challenging environment without it. In a crisis, it helps to isolate the emotional component from the serious task at hand, thereby allowing you to retain perspective and sound judgment. Humor is essential for mental survival and peak performance. Plus, humor drives optimism and a positive attitude. There is no downside, unless it is used to put down, insult, or degrade another. Then it is harmful and counterproductive.

Find Something to Laugh About

I can honestly say that there has never been a day, no matter how tough or tragic, where I couldn't find something to laugh about. I've also never been in a jet where my jaw didn't hurt from trying to laugh with an oxygen mask on. Laughing is therapeutic—and if used properly, it is an unbelievable morale multiplier.

From my earliest days in a fighter squadron, humor, playful pranks, and elaborate practical jokes were expected. In some squadrons we would be required to start each brief or lecture with a joke. On deployments, prior to when satellite TV and the internet were made available to us, the only time we would get everyone in the ready room at the same time was when we were going to show a funny movie. We'd watch the good ones time and time again and commit the best lines to memory. If any of us found an opportunity to use the "line of the moment" in a radio transmission, those of us who heard it would be momentarily paralyzed with laughter.

Movies such as *Weird Science, Uncle Buck,* and *Austin Powers: International Man of Mystery* were treasure troves for memorable lines. When popular TV sitcoms were in vogue, one of our spouses would record them and send them in a care package. When the package arrived, we immediately organized a screening and presented it to record crowds. People from other squadrons would show up uninvited. We had to have alternate screenings for those who were flying. I saw most of *Cheers* and *Seinfeld* episodes in this very manner. In between the care packages and movies, we would be left to devise playful pranks. Some pilots were better at it than others.

Pranking with the Best

"Thumper" was the absolute best prankster. He was creative and disciplined. He wasn't the gregarious "let's get everyone together to pull this off" kind of prankster. He worked in the shadows and mostly alone. The first prank of his that I recall involved our intelligence officer, "Sony." We were all roommates in a seven-person bunk room on board the USS *Enterprise*. On this particular day, the mail plane had just arrived. (For perspective, it normally took three to four weeks for a package to reach us after it had been mailed from the US.) After the plane landed, we'd normally give it about two to three hours and then go down to the ready room to see if we received something. One person always seemed to receive packages: Sony. This day was no different. As good roommates, we brought back his package to our room since he was on watch.

Later, while lying in our bunks, we heard Sony stroll in. Then we heard him opening his package. Within moments we heard him say aloud, "Why would my mom send me hamburgers?" That got our attention. Sure enough, there were two relatively unspoiled hamburgers wrapped in a napkin with condiment packets. Disgusted, Sony choked back a little vomit, threw them out, and went through the rest of the package. There were no other surprises and nothing else looked suspicious (due to Thumper's meticulous rewrapping technique).

On the next mail run, our man Sony received another package, pristine in every way, just like its predecessor. However, this time, in addition to the hamburgers, Thumper included a bonus surprise—pornographic magazines. If Sony suspected a prank, up until now he hadn't let on. He again wondered out loud, "Why would my mom send me such a disgusting care package?" The whole thing went in the trash and concluded that round of pranks. It was interesting to watch as Sony approached, inspected, and opened each package that followed.

Cautious is probably an understatement. We were forever on guard for a Thumper-style hit.

Dark Humor Can Be Some of the Best Humor

I would be lying if I told you that we didn't find humor in tragedy as well—at least in some of the surrounding or tangential circumstances. My first real exposure to this brand of humor happened on my first deployment.

It was summer, it was hot, and we weren't flying very much when we found ourselves in a very dismal and depressing situation on board the USS *Enterprise* operating in the Indian Ocean about 1,000 miles from Diego Garcia as part of our global presence mission. Most of us had been going a week or longer without a precious "trap"—the slang used for a ship-arrested landing and the only relief aircrew typically had from the monotony and tedium of deployment. There is nothing more frustrating on deployment than not flying. We were constantly comparing who had the most "traps" on cruise. As the schedules officer, I was the one responsible for maintaining equity. Everyone was angry at me, and as this condition persisted, tensions grew . . . and then the air conditioning went out.

One day we noticed a lot of commotion near the nuclear reactor access and for a while we were sequestered in the ready room. It was right next to the entrance that led to the ship's nuclear propulsion system, which included eight nuclear reactors. It was also across from the officers' ward room, the term ships use for the place where officers' meals are prepared and served. When the emergency response ended, we were allowed to go to the ward room for our evening meal.

We soon found out that a sailor had died while on watch in one of the reactor rooms. Apparently, as he migrated between compartments in his head-to-toe nuclear-biochemical protection suit, he vomited into his respirator for some unknown reason. Without any way to clear his only breathing option, and with little time and no support to shed his suit, he choked on his own vomit, asphyxiated, and couldn't be revived when help arrived.

As we sat down to eat, a group of corpsmen carried the victim's body right past us to place him in a space that had been cleared for him in the freezer.

There are not very many ways to preserve a body for mortuary services on an aircraft carrier in the Indian Ocean in the summer. We felt horrible for this young man and his family, and we were fully supportive of treating his remains with dignity and respect, even if that meant placing him in the walk-in freezer.

We assumed his stay in the freezer would only be for a day at most. I said a prayer for him and his family and went back to the ready room to finish writing the flight schedule. It was pretty easy since there was only one flight: A US-3 aircraft was scheduled to fly from Diego Garcia to pick up the sailor's body and take him home.

We had a nice memorial service for him the next day, and since we were so close to his temporary morgue in the freezer, we watched a few of his closest shipmates carry him, secured in a standard body bag, to the flight deck for his trip to Diego Garcia, just as the US-3 was about to land. After the plane refueled, dropped off mail (another package for Sony, I think), and the flight crew got something to eat, they prepared for an immediate launch. US-3 pilots were not qualified to land on the ship at night, so they needed to take off sufficiently early to allow them to return to the ship, just in case an emergency situation developed before it got dark. It was a sad and somber launch, knowing that a deceased sailor was making his way back to his family.

I went back to work on another no-fly schedule. Morale was low. As I waited for the CO to sign the schedule, I heard the emergency tones and signals and then an announcement saying the US-3 was coming back. The airplane had a system failure, and with nowhere else to land, was returning to the ship. By the time we were having another meal, our dead shipmate was making his way back to the freezer, awaiting repairs on his ride.

The following day, US-3 number two arrived with the right parts and the right people to fix US-3 number one. Our poor shipmate made another assisted trip to the flight deck and was strapped into US-3 number two. This time, though, he had live passengers with him. This particular airplane is cramped to begin with, and with limited seating, it must have been very awkward for the living passengers. They taxied to the catapult, launched, and within moments had to return to the ship!

The murmurs started in all the other ready rooms. "The dead guy is getting more flight time and traps than we are . . . wow . . . only in the Navy, I guess." Our poor dead shipmate made another return trip to his freezer. But now he was a celebrity. During the past week, he had the most flight time and the most traps in the entire air wing. Everyone was now tracking his status. With no disrespect intended, everyone saw the comical absurdity in this situation, and it served as both a distraction and a morale spark when everyone galvanized together in getting him home.

There would be a third launch and return—I can't recall the reason. But the dead sailor became the only thing anyone talked about. It was so crazy that laughter seemed to be the only option. Humorous cartoons started circulating. Bets were being waged on how many traps he would get and on which flight he would successfully escape his freezer home. On a typical deployment of that era, the average pilot would get about one hundred traps. Since our flying was so limited, we were way off pace. And as each day went by, a dead man was catching up to us. Senior leadership saw this as a mission that had to be solved permanently at the very next opportunity. I suspect the flight crew was instructed to keep heading for Diego Garcia no matter what happened to their jet after they launched. But it would take another couple of days before the next flight. I guess they wanted to make sure the airplane was perfect.

It ended up being kind of like the Super Bowl. You could hear conversations in the passageway predicting the outcome. There were expert commentators who professed to know something about the nature of the previous airplane problems and the prospects of a successful launch. Every ready room had a map hung that highlighted the route to Diego Garcia and the exact point, halfway, where the airplane would turn around when it experienced any problems. Squadrons posted people in Air Operations, where all decisions related to airborne aircraft were made, so they could listen to the communications and give updates to their respective squadrons. There are nine squadrons in a typical air wing, so the crowd was huge.

By now, after three attempts, the move of the body and staging were much more covert. If anyone could have detected it, it would have been our ready room, and we didn't see anything. But when we found out there was only one US-3 launching that day, it was pretty easy to tell when they were getting ready to go. All eyes were glued to the flight deck camera video via the thousands of TVs available throughout the enormous ship. The airplane taxied and was connected to the catapult. No apparent problems. The airplane went to full power, and the flight controls were cycled. Still no problems. The catapult officer saluted the pilot, cleared the airspace ahead, and touched the flight deck, signifying the catapult operator to push the go button. Many of the people on the flight deck moved toward the catapult to salute our comrade and pay their final respects.

The catapult fired, and within moments the airplane was airborne and turning toward Diego Garcia. I've made that ride before in the same type of aircraft, from about the same location. We estimated it would take about six hours for the US-3 to arrive at Diego Garcia. We hit our timers and waited.

At one hour, everything was normal. There were no weather issues or aircraft issues. They continued on track. At two hours, the radios started to get scratchy and hard to understand, but they were still on track. Just prior to the three-hour mark, we lost radio contact with them. It was assumed that they weren't coming back, but we couldn't be absolutely sure until they reported safe on deck. That would be another three hours.

Finally, with patience running thin and a whole ship fixated on this single event, we got word that our dead shipmate was not coming back to the USS *Enterprise*. He was on his way back home to his family where he belonged. His final trap count, if memory serves me correctly, stood at three. In retrospect, I imagine that our departed friend would be quite proud of himself. The circumstances of his death and the events that followed it made a direct and positive impact on the shipmates he left behind. We had been in the doldrums. He changed that. Our morale had been low. He changed that. Everyone was focused on their own suffering rather than their blessings. He changed that too. Humor is a powerful thing.

★★★

I think George Bernard Shaw got it right when he observed, "Life does not cease to be funny when people die any more than it ceases to be serious when people laugh."

When I'm having a tough day or those around me are, I am quick to reflect on my worst days as a fighter pilot but find it hard to continue to do so. My data retrieval is quickly derailed and is immediately replaced by reflections of joy, exhilaration, camaraderie, gut-wrenching laughter, accomplishment, and shameless fun. The organization I belonged to had a wonderful internal control system that mostly kept humility, grace, likability, and humor fashionable. Perhaps there are some people who don't understand the importance or relevance of being grounded this way, but it is an important element of my parenting that was discovered and nurtured in my development as a fighter pilot.

In my family, we all have call signs, and we are all quick to bring each other back to earth when necessary. We love to laugh, and we seldom have problems laughing at ourselves.

But the premium placed long ago on humility, grace, likability, and humor predates my fighter pilot generation, so I give credit to those Americans who understood the intrinsic value that these qualities bring and had the wisdom to infuse those legacy values into our traditions and culture. I can't help but think that it has saved a lot of lives and produced many wonderful, likeable, and successful Americans.

Having moved several times in my military career, these particular attributes ended up being extremely valuable to my kids as they were forced to figure out how to fit in, make new friends, and earn the respect and trust of others in each new school and community through which we migrated. They are truly masters at it now in their own particular ways.

✭✭✭

 **FIGHTER PILOT PARENT TAKEAWAYS—
Likability, Humility, Grace, and Humor**

✭ Make your children feel welcome when they ask you for help with schoolwork or other challenges.

✭ Never withhold grace from your kids except when extending grace would negatively impact family morale or add an unacceptable risk.

✭ When you correct your children, do so without anger or revenge, and with your aim being to improve them.

✭ If a child suffers from low confidence, remind them of their successes and accomplishments, and compare their journey with others that have gone before them.

✭ When you need to balance overconfidence, recalibrate your child's version of reality and encourage them to think through all the possible obstacles that they can and can't control. Sometimes experience may be the only thing that works.

✭ Find a way to bring family members back to earth when necessary. Laughing at and with each other is a great way to do this.

CHAPTER SIX

THE FUN FACTOR

———

L ife is hard. Work is hard. School is hard. Anything worth doing is generally challenging and hard. Can it be fun too? Absolutely! It needs to be, or you just may stop doing what you are passionate about.

Naval aviation wrestles all the time with the problem of how to keep things fun amid the challenges and hard work. We've experienced cycles where retention, especially in fighter squadrons, becomes extremely low. Normally a retention plunge is expected when economic conditions and opportunity are favorable outside of the military service sector. There is also a strong correlation when there is a drop in the quantity and quality of flight time. But when those two factors aren't issues, it becomes a challenge to explain why a group of people would leave the profession they love and have sacrificed dearly for. In the late 1990s, we were faced with this exact dilemma.

It was during this period that I first started focusing on the term "fun factor." In exit interviews, it became apparent that a certain something related to fun was not sufficiently present. OK, great. But what was it exactly that people were missing? Since fun meant different things to different people, it was really hard to quantify.

Generally speaking, when you remove the opportunity for creativity, limit friendly competition, and place lots of senseless rules and standards on participants, the fun factor will diminish.

That's common sense, or so it would seem.

The challenge is to make challenging, arduous work fun. Fun work is the most rewarding and satisfying. Fun work is something you look forward to. And if done right, fun work accelerates skill mastery and IQ. And from fun work comes the biggest and most important bonus— elevated teamwork, camaraderie, and esprit de corps.

In the late '90s, the fun factor issue became so significant that the commander of naval air forces met with his commanding officers to discuss solutions. The list of potential factors contributing to dissatisfaction was long:

☆ The Cold War had ended, which resulted in a reduction in funding for flight operations and the military in general; less flight time; and the absence of a "bad" guy to go up against.

☆ Political correctness went well beyond what was needed.

☆ Inflexibility became pervasive.

☆ There was a culture shift from Baby Boomers to Generation X to Millennials. (In other words, Baby Boomers didn't get the younger generations or how they perceived the world.)

In reality, though, it was probably a complex set of factors that conjoined at about the same time to create a very low-fun environment.

As I write this, it sounds ridiculous: How could there have been a low-fun environment when you're flying a high-performance jet? How could you not have fun when the view from your office was from 25,000 feet? How could you not have fun wearing green pajamas to work every day? How could you not have fun blowing things up?

Well, we blew up lots of brain cells thinking of how we could bring the fun factor back and sustain it. And we wanted to figure it out, because sadly we weren't having fun figuring out how to have more fun.

Dangerous Fun and Rewarding Fun

From my perspective, there are really two kinds of fun. One is useless and dangerous. The other is healthy and rewarding. The dangerous fun leaves destruction in its wake. Rewarding fun builds high-performing teams.

Let's talk about useless and dangerous fun first. This is the kind of fun that parents and commanding officers worry about. This is where overconfidence plays a big role. Rules, common sense, and even the laws of physics are negotiable to these fun seekers. Flying at 600 knots, 200 feet above the ground, and dropping bombs just isn't enough for everyone. Some idiots, of which I was one in my early years, feel they had to do crazy things (like dip a tailhook in the water) to maximize the fun factor. For me, though, my little indiscretion was the opposite of fun. I didn't feel any elation—only guilt.

Another form of dangerous fun comes from mission creep. It includes those who attempt to perform missions they're not trained for or their aircraft isn't designed for. They can quickly find themselves hopelessly in over their head or beyond the structural limits of the aircraft. It's kind of like a skier trying to snowboard. Only bad things can happen.

Whatever the dangerous fun, there is always a purposeful violation of a rule, procedure, instruction, or common sense. We called it giving yourself a personal waiver. Those waivers are often deadly in aviation.

Like a drug, once the personal waivers start, the demand for more can become insatiable for certain personalities. Sure, they'll scare themselves every once in a while, or they may even get caught and reprimanded. But after laying low for a bit, the itch comes back.

When I think about all the dangerous fun-factor mishaps I observed, three prominent factors were always present.

Personal Waiver Conditions

○ First, a "compromised" pilot would find himself alone or with a very junior pilot who would be uncomfortable saying anything contradictory to the superior pilot.

○ Second, the mission was either vague or extremely flexible.

○ Third, the pilot had a lot of extra gas to burn.

In a parenting situation, this would be the equivalent of having an adventurous child who is unsupervised, dropped off without a specific plan, and armed with a pocketful of cash. The potential for dangerous fun goes way up when all those factors are present.

Understanding the Threshold

Without a plan and no supervision, everything a vulnerable person has contemplated doing or imagined doing is now possible and, they may think, risk-free. With a jet at their disposal and lots of gas, they have the means to pull it off. Here is where knowing your personnel (pilots or kids) is so important. As individuals, each of us has a unique and independent propensity toward dangerous fun and fun-factor fulfillment. Understanding where that threshold exists and having a feel for any aggravating factors that lead to it will allow you to put controls and supervision in place for your child, just as I tried to do with pilots. Failing to do so will up the risk.

To illustrate, I'd like to share the tragic story of a very close friend of mine who failed to return from a flight one summer day.

At the time, I was the air wing safety officer flying with one of the two F/A-18 squadrons. The air wing was in between deployments, and the squadrons were responsible for their own local training in Lemoore, California, where they shared a hangar. I received notification from my friend's squadron that they had activated their mishap plan after he was an hour late for his land time. I immediately went down to the squadron to assist.

I learned that my friend was on a solo flight—with no wingman. He had been tasked with checking out an airplane that had just been returned to the flight schedule after a significant maintenance procedure. If the jet was good, he was then going to intercept a flight of his squadron's airplanes that were on a low-altitude training route. His plan was to sneak up on them and quickly test their ability to visually scan for air threats before proceeding home. The whole mission should have taken only fifteen minutes out of a ninety-minute flight. When you deducted his transit time, the balance of forty minutes would be his free time.

Not long after the mishap response team gathered, we started receiving reports of a fire in the vicinity of a popular recreational area on the east side of the Sierra Nevada, about five miles from where the low-level planes would have seen him. This was not a good sign. We launched another flight to verify what was being reported, and if necessary, provide on-scene support to assist with rescue. It didn't take long to confirm the worst. With a blazing fire and aircraft debris discovered at the end of a steep canyon, it was apparent we had lost an aircraft. Now we had to figure out what the pilot's status was.

Eyewitnesses reported seeing an aircraft—flying at extremely low altitude and high speed—enter the canyon from west to east. From a pilot's perspective, the canyon was pretty cool. It was steep on both sides but wide enough that two aircraft could fly next to one another at low altitude. There was one tricky part, though. About seven or eight miles into it, the canyon took an abrupt ninety-degree left turn to the north and then came to an immediate end. At high airspeeds, you would need to use an extremely aggressive turn to avoid hitting the canyon sides, and as soon as you completed the turn, you would need to pull up hard to avoid crashing into the canyon wall.

The plane was discovered near an outcropping near the end of the canyon. No ejection or parachute had been reported. After our mishap team arrived on site, we found the pilot's remains pretty close to the rock outcropping. He had not attempted an ejection.

He was a good, respected, and experienced pilot. What could we possibly tell his wife and children? The mishap lingo we typically used for this type of accident—controlled flight into terrain (CFIT)—just didn't seem like a great or respectful option for his grieving family.

As in all mishap investigations, we collected physical evidence, interviewed squadron personnel, looked at the pilot's health and routine from the previous seventy-two hours, and then tried to identify every factor that might have led to his death. Meanwhile, his friends and family agonized, memorials were planned and executed, and a young, fatherless family started thinking about how they would put their lives back together.

The investigation into the crash started to provide clues.

After all the parts of the airplane that created movement, such as ailerons and rudders, were analyzed, nothing seemed amiss. After all the maintenance records and maintenance procedures were reviewed, nothing was out of place. All the witnesses reported that there were no fires or explosions prior to impact. After combining all this evidence, we were confident that the plane had been in perfect working order. There were no other aircraft in the area at the time of the mishap, so there were no traffic conflicts. We needed to look somewhere else.

Eventually, the investigation team decided to use another jet to video the route at precisely the same time of day and at approximately the same altitude and airspeed as the mishap aircraft. In the F/A-18, a camera records everything the pilot sees. We also had pictures taken from the same angle but at ground level and at different times of the day. The clues began to emerge from the video and the pictures. It became clear that the rock outcropping where the jet made first contact with the ground basically disappeared visually for a very narrow span of time each afternoon. That particular time period perfectly coincided with the mishap flight.

So, from the initial analysis, we knew the aircraft was fine, and we knew there was an optical illusion. It was also clear that if the pilot had been flying at the minimal allowed altitudes, the rock outcropping wouldn't have been an issue.

A Tragic Personal Waiver

The next part of the investigation was where things got interesting. As we started interviewing other pilots, a fun-factor theme started to emerge. Apparently this was not the first time my friend had flown through the canyon at low altitude. He had done it many times before, sometimes with fairly junior wingmen. The pilots who had made this canyon run with him before were uncomfortable—and then scared—when both the altitude and the airspeed became more aggressive and unsafe. The wingmen eventually were forced to pull up and out of the canyon for fear of their lives. Because it was a senior pilot who was leading them astray, they had been hesitant to say anything. These personal waivers thus became a tragic and well-kept secret in the squadron.

All the ingredients were present for dangerous fun. We had an independent pilot with a vague mission, lots of gas, and a history of personal waivers. Witnesses also reported that he had made several runs before the impact. We speculated that on each successive run, while he was waiting for his squadron mates on their low-altitude training route, he incrementally reduced his altitude and increased his speed. And as he got lower and faster, the sun angle gradually changed, eventually blending the rock outcropping into the background, making it invisible to him on his last pass. If he had adhered to all the rules pertaining to altitude (1,500 feet above the ground while solo), and airspeed (250 knots below 10,000 feet unless on an approved training route), this would have never happened. The desire for dangerous fun was too strong for him to resist.

Based on this single mishap and the loss of my close friend, I made significant changes in the way I managed those three significant contributing factors (solo, mission, and gas) in the future. First, as a supervisor, I would try to schedule two aircraft together at a minimum. Not only was this how we deployed and fought, but this was also the best way to provide mutual support. I consider this absolutely indispensable.

"It creates something of a contract between honorable and professional peers or kids and parents."

I would also strive to really know our personnel and create pairings that would reduce dangerous fun-factor risks (using the buddy system and indirect supervision). If single aircraft flights couldn't be avoided, the pilot of a single aircraft would brief his intended mission in detail to the duty officer (the who, when, where, what, how, and why details). Most people seem to have a very strong tendency to do exactly what they tell others they are going to do. It creates something of a contract between honorable and professional peers or kids and parents. And finally, every flight would brief in detail alternate missions or backup contingencies for situations when the main objective could not be accomplished. It worked very well.

This also informed my approach to fun-factor parenting. When it comes to dangerous fun risk management, I don't like my children going anywhere by themselves. Even if they don't have much of a dangerous fun-factor gene, it is still better to have the mutual support of other friends or siblings. My wife and I try to know the "personnel" involved as well. Certain friends bring unacceptable risk. Certain adults bring unacceptable risk too. We insist on knowing the friends and sometimes the family before we'll commit to a potentially risky endeavor. And finally, we go over their timelines in detail. Time, place, intentions, transportation, and mobility are all discussed. Our kids—and yours—are just too precious to leave these things to chance or fate. Plus, as parents, we strive to model the same behaviors we expect in our kids. We let each other know where we're going, when we'll be there, and then we communicate any changes to the plan. Informal contracts are powerful dangerous fun modifiers.

> "Plus, as parents, we strive to model the same behaviors we expect in our kids."

When Fun Is Not Fun

The world is awash with traditions and ceremonies that have become nothing more than an excuse for retribution, hazing, or personal vendettas. The Navy is no different. This type of "fun" needs to be crushed. It's a recipe for disaster and a cause for low morale. Hazing can be "fun" for some, but it is always embarrassing, humiliating, and occasionally even dangerous for the person who is targeted. In my career, I've come across people who were stripped naked and helplessly taped to a cart or chair with beer bottles taped to their hands and their eyebrows shaved. What purpose does this type of behavior serve?

Hazing, Initiations, Games, and Other Traditions

The Navy has lots of traditions where abuses can find fertile ground.

We have the Crossing the Line/Shellback Ceremony that occurs while crossing the equator and basically involves forcing people to crawl around in smelly muck. Then there is the Blue or Red Nose Ceremony while crossing the Arctic Circle or Antarctic Circle, which entails doing the same thing as the Shellback Ceremony but under much colder conditions.

Then there are all the initiations—solo flight, winging, chief, and officer promotions. The list is endless, but occasionally things can get out of hand. Some traditions don't even involve physical pain, suffering, or discomfort. For some, money, or the lack of it, can be an equally embarrassing or humiliating situation.

When air wings get together for training, it's common for the whole group to gather at the Officers' Club. And when together, it is also common to employ multiple 200-year-old strategies to get others to pay for drinks. Of course, nuggets (new guys) are the most frequent victims.

One important tradition—and one that most nuggets learn the hard way—is to never enter the bar with your hat on. If you do, and if you are detected, the bell behind the bar is rung, and you are then obligated to buy everyone at the bar a drink. That could be anywhere from 100 to 300 drinks—the equivalent of a two-month paycheck for a new guy!

The Real Fun

Now that we have the dangerous and not-fun fun out of the way, let's talk about real fun. This is the type of fun that creates no real losers, humiliates no one, and enhances rather than compromises safety and camaraderie.

I've learned that people (and especially kids) love games and competition. As long as the game or competition is fair, and everyone has a chance to contribute and be successful, fun-factor points can be very high.

On deployment, we would have friendly competitions for just about everything. There were mustache-growing contests, weight-loss contests, and once we even had weight-gain contests for the emaciated. There were eating contests for both volume and grossness. If there was a way to compete, we'd find it. Back home, our spouses would take pictures of their feet, eyes, knees, or other appropriate body parts at close range, and we'd have competitions guessing who they belonged to. Our spouses would also compete back home in bed races, fundraising, and other community events as a form of moral support for us and other military families. This was good, healthy, clean fun. Everyone won.

On the tactical side, every time we dropped bombs, we had competitions for the best first bomb, best overall bomb, best average bomb, and even best direct hits. We would compete either as teams or as individuals. Losers would buy winners Cokes. But for naval aviation, there is one competition that stands out far above all the others—aircraft carrier landing grades.

If you could place value and importance on every single fighter pilot skill, one skill overshadows all others: the pilot boarding rate—the percentage of ship landings to attempts. It's kind of like free throw percentages in basketball. The "Shaqs" of naval aviation were a huge liability. The second most valuable skill was landing performance, and with landing performance having such exulted status, high visibility, and importance in naval aviation, this is where pilots vigorously compete to be the best.

As you would imagine, experienced pilots perform better than nugget pilots. What is not so obvious, though, is that squadrons with better aircraft and better maintenance teams also perform better. Aircraft with better and more reliable systems can make a significant difference and give pilots a distinct advantage during landing.

Now for the fun factor. Before a squadron ever arrives at the ship, competitive teams are formed that spread pilot experience between them. The teams also include maintenance, ordnance, administrative and supply officers—everybody gets in on the fun.

After arriving on the ship, the very first item unpacked and hung on the wall is the greenie board. The competition period is then set, usually ending just before the next port visit. The board is updated every day, and as it becomes increasingly colored (with green signifying good—hence "greenie board"—and red/orange signifying bad), it starts to become the focal point for all visitors.

Teammates cheer each other on, and a few of them are usually nearby when the LSOs come by to debrief a landing. This is the kind of competition that gets everyone involved, and it also motivates both pilots and technicians to achieve a higher level of performance.

What about the pilots that were having serious landing problems? How did this competition affect them? Should they be treated differently or even excused from the competition?

For a struggling pilot, the added pressure of a highly visible competition can be overwhelming. In my early days, I can remember being fixated on the greenie board. When I knew I would be flying at night, I couldn't think of anything else, no matter how hard I tried. Then, if I ended up having a "bad" landing, I would also be totally fixated on the nasty orange or red square by my name on the greenie board the next day. To make matters worse, as an LSO-in-training, I was also the one responsible for coloring the board.

You might think it would be tempting to remove a struggling pilot from the board temporarily to avoid public humiliation and to focus on improvement, but that just introduces much more pressure, and it still doesn't improve performance. Since all landings are broadcast to every TV on the ship, most people already know who is having a problem. In some extreme cases, when a known struggling pilot is scheduled for a night trap, it is not uncommon for everybody to stop what they are doing, pause the movies and the pranks, and tune in to watch the show. They've all been there before, so it's sort of a weird combination of curiosity and solidarity. With each attempt (there are usually many), cheers, shrieks, and yells can be heard from all the ready rooms as the drama builds. Then, when the options are to either divert or get more gas from another aircraft configured to transfer fuel, the plane successfully lands and the show finally ends.

As embarrassing as it is to be struggling publicly like that, having your name removed from the greenie board is much worse. For close-knit teams, it's like being excommunicated or being told you're not part of the family. It's a symbolic rejection of the worse kind. Having your name still on the board, with all its colorful orange and red highlights, at least shows that your teammates still believe in you and know you will overcome. Sometimes, no matter how bad you feel for someone who is struggling, you just have to let the struggling run its course and support them through it. All competitions eventually end, and as long as you're not dangerous, you will get a fresh chance at redemption the next time. The sun will rise again.

At the end of this landing competition, grades are tallied, and a winner is announced. The winning team enjoys both the celebrity status of winning as well as the benefit of a free dinner on the losers. From there, everyone updates their handicap, teams are reshuffled, and the competition begins anew. The losers have nowhere to go but up.

> " . . . fun-factor competitions are only useful and healthy if they are fair, relate to an important skill, and make everyone involved feel like a contributor."

In summary, fun-factor competitions are only useful and healthy if they are fair, relate to an important skill, and make everyone involved feel like a contributor. Any lesser framework will kill the fun factor for some, if not all. As a parent, if you're creative, you can always find ways to apply this concept for whatever your kids are involved in. With the fun factor, participant energy, focus, and attitude are optimized. If you're doing it right, kids don't want to stop; they are literally shocked when it ends and beg for more.

Seeing this work so effectively for Navy fighter pilots and my family, I started using it for youth sports as a coach.

Keep the Fun Factor High

With kids, there is nothing more frustrating than not being successful when you try something new. You can tell them to keep trying and they'll eventually get it, but "eventually" is a long time for a kid. If you want them to keep trying and not give up, the fun factor must be extremely high.

It is the fun factor that makes them prepare, practice, and try harder, just like their Navy fighter pilot counterparts. It all starts with building fun into the plan for achieving success. For this to work, they need to experience immediate success. A taste of success creates an appetite for more challenge. When they see results, they are then ready for competition.

As a youth lacrosse coach, I couldn't get the fun-factor concept out of my head. I immediately looked for ways to leverage fun the way I did when I was designing fighter training plans. A fighter training plan starts with learning objectives, then adds events and challenges that make the training realistic as well as fun.

Of the thousands of drills or activities I could possibly use as a coach, I started breaking each one down by age/skill level, position, conditioning factor, touch rate factor, skill attainment, speed factor, game-like factor, and—most importantly—fun factor. Each attribute was scored for each activity or drill. For comparable drills, the ones that were lacking in the fun factor generally produced the lowest focus and intensity, and therefore, the lowest results. The fun factor was also highly correlated with touch rate and game-like factors. As I did with the best fighter training plans, I stopped using low fun-factor drills altogether or modified them to achieve a higher fun-factor result.

When I started converting old training plans to plans with heavily weighted fun-factor components, adjusted for age and skill level, I discovered that my players didn't want practice to end. From my point of view, that is the best metric around for training effectiveness. Their learning rate soared, and when comparing results throughout a season, it was striking how much they advanced compared to their competition. When I drifted from that model, a falloff in performance and morale followed.

"If you spend the time thinking about it, you can turn anything into a competitive game with high fun factor."

If you spend the time thinking about it, you can turn anything into a competitive game with high fun factor. You just have to be a little creative. The great teachers, coaches, instructors, and leaders of the world have a firm grasp of this important concept. My family participates in several family sports activities at the local basketball court. With ages spanning forty-five years, and with a significant variation in skill and experience, we can still create a fun factor by handicapping the better players (limiting what they can do, for example) and creating pairings that allow for friendly competition. From soccer to basketball to tennis, we simultaneously focus on success management for the weaker or younger players while challenging the better players in areas where they wouldn't normally challenge themselves.

As a parent, you can and should use the fun-factor approach at home. More importantly, you should definitely demand that the people you depend on to develop your children toward their passions also deploy the fun factor in a useful and healthy way. When a kid comes home from school or practice excited to share something they did, it is normally due to the fun factor. When they don't want to go to practice or they don't like a particular subject at school, even if they're gifted at it, the fun factor is typically missing.

"When a kid comes home from school or practice excited to share something they did, it is normally due to the fun factor."

My kids have become masters at the fun factor. My daughters are incredibly good with children, and they always seem to distinguish themselves as the most popular babysitters and youth coaches. They have learned how to leverage the fun factor into multiple leadership and teaching positions, using games and competition to optimize teaching, learning, and behavior. It has become a natural part of their personality.

Challenge, Innovation, Creativity, and Spontaneity

The next healthy fun-factor piece involves challenge, innovation, creativity, and spontaneity. I've had my share of fun in a jet, but those extra-fun moments have always happened when we were faced with manageable yet challenging surprises. In all family competitions and coaching situations, I will routinely throw in wild-card challenges when things become too easy or predictable. It could be as simple as removing participants for a short period of time, but the objective is for them to quickly think their way through a mitigation plan. Those special situations really elevate the competitive fun factor because they are always forced to apply their team's skills and talents in a unique and creative way to overcome an unplanned tactical problem or surprise. In other words, they have to spontaneously respond to an unscripted situation. They have to make quick decisions.

One of the two most fun training flights I've ever experienced was the Top Gun 1v1 graduation flight I mentioned in Chapter Two. Even though I was exhausted that day and so not in top form, the flight itself had all the key fun-factor attributes: It was competitive, realistic, challenging, and leveraged uncertainty to incite tactical creativity and innovation. It produced almost the same physiological responses as real combat. I got butterflies as I started reviewing in my mind all the tactical possibilities and proper counters.

When in training, other than knowing that they will be fighting one of the top pilots in the fleet, pilots know nothing else of tactical significance. They can't really create and execute a plan of attack until the moment they first see their adversary. Everything they've learned about threat airplanes, threat tactics, threat weapons, airspeed, and angles must instantaneously fuse into an offensive, neutral, or defensive game plan. Failure to see the other guy first will usually end badly.

Failure to recognize the key visual cues and corresponding tactical options will put them at a disadvantage, as will failure to think three or four steps ahead.

Events like this really add high fun-factor value. Unlike most scripted training, adding uncertainty brings a special level of sophistication that develops critical mental skills and produces quick and innovative responses when faced with surprises or adversity. Instead of fear and meltdowns when things get out of hand or overwhelming, pilots have confidence in their training and are rewarded with composure and good responses.

The second most fun training flight I've experienced is very similar except it involved a wingman and a much larger uncertainty factor. Adding a partner in crime and allocating responsibilities between each other introduces another important fun-factor ingredient: using team creativity to solve uncertainty challenges that can't possibly be solved alone.

The setup for this training flight was pretty simple. It involved two aircraft responsible for defending a fifteen mile by fifteen mile volume of air from the surface to 25,000 feet. In that airspace, there are also one or more threat aircraft trying to kill the pilots (simulated, of course). The pilots don't know where the threat aircraft are or from where they will attack. Without initial cueing, they are literally vulnerable in all quadrants around them. This scenario also requires visually identifying any aircraft as hostile before shooting them. This is very challenging.

There are three ways to find the bad guys: visually, on radar, or by threat sensors if they are tracking you on their radar. The way the training is set up, the bad guys usually find the good guys first.

Success in this very defensive and uncertain environment depends on how the team can optimize its tools and tactics to detect the threat as early as possible, maneuver to defend and counter, and then finish them off.

The best teams are disciplined about searching in their own separate small areas to cover a much larger area with their combined eyes and radars. The best teams creatively orient to the threat, once they detect it, using standard tactics. The best teams creatively communicate roles and responsibilities to each other to either defend and counter—or attack. The best teams creatively kill the threat in the least amount of time. The best teams help each other achieve the highest situational awareness through communication. Unlike the Top Gun 1v1 event, wingman performance and contribution are often the other uncertainty factors that must be accounted for. Creatively achieving high mutual support makes all the difference in the world. Not only does this type of training punch every fun-factor ticket, but you also learn to work as a team.

"We could make up a game out of thin air, and we became quite good at innovating for age, weather, and darkness."

When I pull this back into parenting and coaching, I pine for the days of my youth. Today it seems as if most every child activity is planned and scripted. They have playdates and highly controlled, highly organized activities. When I was a kid, we made up our own games and improvised when we didn't have all the proper gear. We could make up a game out of thin air, and we became quite good at innovating for age, weather, and darkness.

When Things Don't Work Out

When those all-important fun-factor components of spontaneity, creativity, and uncertainty are missing, it is tough to learn how to be successful when things don't turn out as expected. When I work with kids, I like to bring in controlled chaos and uncertainty as part of what we do. I want kids to learn how to think on their feet and innovate in response to unexpected conditions. The infusion of unanticipated wild-card elements that change the nature of the competition really helps kids manage uncertainty, chaos, and teamwork. It could be something as simple as adding time pressure to a scenario.

When I do this with kids who were brought up in very scripted and predictable controlled environments, they absolutely hate it . . . initially. They hate it because they don't know how to respond to uncertainty.

"They hate it because they don't know how to respond to uncertainty."

Because they don't anticipate it, they don't have a winning strategy ready to go and therefore become easily frustrated because they don't know what to do. What they fail to realize is that they truly have all the tools they need to evolve quickly if they want to. If you want kids to adapt well and even thrive in dynamic environments, fun-factor exposures must also include dynamic surprises that get them out of their comfort zone.

Eventually, as they learn how to adapt to uncertainty and develop their creative side, the light bulb slowly comes on. And when it goes on, they can't get enough of it because their fun factor eventually skyrockets.

Some of the most enjoyable moments come when I let kids create their own chaos and uncertainty games. It forces them to think about how they would use their skills in unique situations. It lets them be the same kind of kid I remember being—the kid without all the organization and controls. The only condition I place on them is that whatever they come up with has to be new and different and honor the game. Creativity is a beautiful thing and really elevates the fun factor.

Random Acts of Kindness

The last fun-factor concept I'll share is especially personal with me. I defy anyone to argue that being the recipient of a random act of kindness isn't uplifting and fun. I'll go one step further and suggest that those very acts can change your whole outlook and attitude for days, if not weeks. I'll go even one step beyond that and suggest that those random acts of kindness will propagate themselves well beyond the first wave. It's a fun gift that keeps on giving.

In a squadron, we try to do this with meritorious days off and spot awards for uncommon contributions. The act of kindness is totally unexpected and reflects the love and appreciation for those we depend on. Recipients talk about it for years and years because it is both fun and out of the ordinary.

The first time I tried this out on a large scale with my family, it was a huge success. I was in the local flower shop buying something for my wife when I made the comment that it was too bad that I wouldn't be able to do this next year because I'd be on deployment. "Hold on a second," said the clerk. "There may be another option to consider." She introduced me to a very clever system many other deploying pilots had been using. It had an amazing impact on my wife and daughters.

The florist asked me to think of every birthday, holiday, and special event that would pass while I was deployed. Then she had me throw in some "random acts of kindness" dates for good measure. I came up with twenty to twenty-five dates in all. We then went over to the card display, where I spent the next thirty minutes writing out cards for each and every event.

We then created a file and linked each card to a bouquet, arrangement, or single flower. After another thirty minutes and lots of money, I left, hoping the shop would be true to their promised delivery schedule. Eventually the fateful day arrived, and off I went with my squadron mates, not to be seen again for nine to ten months. The first random act of kindness was scheduled to arrive the very next day.

Like clockwork, the flower shop fulfilled its obligations, and the first of many random acts of kindness found their way to my house. I wish I had been there to see their faces, but from the letters I received, it went over extremely well. The deliveries were timed so that flowers and a card showed up every week or so, and it really took the edge off a long separation and all the associated challenges of a combat deployment. To this day, my wife and daughters still talk about it.

What I didn't calculate was that the word would get out to the other wives. When those wives found out, boy, did their husbands get an earful!

You can't go wrong with the healthy fun-factor approach.

 ## FIGHTER PILOT PARENT TAKEAWAYS— The Fun Factor

☆ Provide an opportunity for challenge, innovation, creativity, and spontaneity to create a high fun factor. My son learned early math very quick on a stationary bike complete with a Scooby-Doo video interface that rewarded him for steering into correct answers. Math is still his favorite subject.

☆ Avoid competition that is limited, unfair, overly structured, or not correlated to a development objective. When we play "h-o-r-s-e" at the local basketball court, we keep it fair by making the best players use their weak shooting hands, and the least accomplished players gets extra shots and a reduced distance.

☆ Camaraderie enhances any fun challenge. I still remember my young daughters' pride and satisfaction when they were rewarded for picking up their toys. Not only did they giggle the whole time, but they figured out ways to work together to reduce the time—which meant bonus prizes.

☆ Avoid leaving your children alone (or with a high-risk partner) without enough structure or supervision, or with abundant or excessive means to execute a dangerous plan. Jeep-Daughter-Van Nuys says it all.

☆ Use games and competitions to produce the highest fun factor and the quickest results. After lacrosse practice, I reward kids who collect the most balls. If I don't make it a game, it takes forever and only a few make an effort, which tends to build resentment.

☆ Make sure all games or competitions are inclusive, fair, and develop a valuable skill. If you start with the end in mind and allow the participants to create the competition, their creativity will surprise you.

☆ Don't over-script. Rules are important, but when I made my lacrosse kids perform a number of skills before they could shoot at the goal in practice, an unintended consequence was that they didn't shoot when they should have during games.

☆ Everything can be turned into a game or competition. My nine-year-old son learned a guitar song in two days and performed the song in public—all so he could download a precious video game.

CHAPTER SEVEN

MANAGING FEAR AND STRESS

——

Fear is essential for survival. It keeps you safe by helping you anticipate and avoid danger. But fear can also inhibit rational thought, good decisions, and optimal performance. When fear is allowed (yes, *you* control *it*) to bend toward the irrational, it can negatively impact everything you do. Fear, if unchecked, can be so paralyzing that it prevents you from thinking or acting in your own best interest or in the best interest of others. It can also be deadly when it adversely imperils time-critical decisions and behaviors. Conquering and mastering of your fears is important and possible, but it takes practice.

As a young pilot, I faced a new fear every day—or so it seemed. It was probably more apprehension than fear, but I was clearly focused on imagining future scenarios that all ended with disappointment, calamity, or setbacks. Having never flown, and with plenty of access to first-hand accounts of every possible bad thing that could happen to student aviators as they progressed through the pipeline, it wasn't too hard to place myself in those situations and imagine the same nasty outcomes. I wasn't really any different from those who had gone before me and failed, *was I*?

Irrational Fear: The Future and the Unknown

The unknown and the future are fertile ground for irrational fear. My first big aviation fear was not being able to pass the pilot eye exam when I first started flight school. I was not alone in my fear. Every one of us obsessed about it. Some went so far as to visit an eye doctor on the side and ask for a pair of magic "vision-enhancing" glasses. Those who explored this option made it sound as though the glasses promoted some sort of eye fitness, like a spin class did for the body. Most of them ended up being disappointed.

We all knew that if we failed the eye exam, the dream of becoming a Navy pilot would end before it began. Since we couldn't study for the exam, we spent lots of time trying not to strain or fatigue our eyes just before the big test. And boy, did we obsess, up to and including the moment we finally received a thumbs-up. That fear averted, I was on to my next challenge: survival swimming.

My naval academy grade point average was easily 0.3 to 0.4 points lower than it should have been as a direct result of my limited aquatic skills. I don't float, and therefore I don't glide. I am inflicted with negative buoyancy. While everyone else would get across the pool in five strokes, it would take me eight. During my four years at school, I ended up barely passing all the timed swimming tests. My only strength, if you could call it that, was my ability to hold my breath and swim under the surface. It makes sense, as I spent quite a bit of time in that position. I was also good at jumping into the water from high distances. I'll give most of the credit for that to gravity, though.

With this backdrop, and with the eye test behind me, I headed toward my next pilot training hurdle. Unlike in *An Officer and a Gentleman,* I'd much rather deal with the underwater obstacles than the surface challenges any day. I was definitely an underwater man. We were expected to tread water for twenty minutes and then "drown proof," a special technique we used to relax and avoid exhaustion in the water, for another ten minutes. We were also required to wear every piece of pilot gear we would normally wear in a jet. The full rig included a flight suit, boots, gloves, harness, g-suit, survival vest, flotation vest (uninflated), helmet, and mask. From an irrational fear perspective, it didn't help much that a student had recently drowned in the weeks leading up to my first attempt, and although I didn't fear drowning that much, I definitely recalculated the level of difficulty with all that gear.

My first attempt was not impressive. I mistakenly thought that my swimming struggles at the naval academy had prepared me well—plus I had been hanging out at the pool quite a bit during my time off. I should have taken notice when instructors lined the pool deck with ten-foot bamboo poles in their hands. On the clock, all forty of us jumped in and began treading. The first twenty seconds were easy. *I've got this,* I thought to myself. After about a minute, the bamboo poles started doing their work. Body after body passed by me, creating a slight wake, as exhausted swimmers were hauled to the side. At two minutes, I was spent. I was so tired I didn't know if I could even reach up and grab the pole. I started to panic. As I became fatigued and my mouth and nose filled with water, I felt a nudge on my flailing hand, and I grabbed for whatever it was that was poking me. In that moment, I discovered what it must feel like to be drowning.

The ride to the edge of the pool, via the bamboo express, was glorious. The relief was indescribable. The bamboo guy was my new best friend. My elation soon turned to depression as I contemplated my future. I needed a tenfold improvement in a week. No problem. I could do this. Off I went.

Sure, I hit the pool every day, but I wasn't seeing any performance improvement. I was too embarrassed to ask for help, so I kept doing the same things I had been doing before, and we know how that turned out. The moment of truth was soon upon me. As I approached the pool deck for the second time, my bamboo buddy from my previous attempt winked at me. I told myself that I'd drown before I grabbed that stupid pole again. In we all went.

As I pushed off from the side, I got busy. I was churning up a storm. A minute passed, and I was still hanging in there. At two minutes, my new personal record, I was doing OK. Passing three minutes, I was starting to struggle a little and moved to the middle of the pool to avoid the temptation of reflexively grabbing at a pole. At four minutes, I found myself in familiar territory—pre-drowning exhaustion. As I maneuvered back to the bamboo sanctuary, I surprisingly felt a little relief, but as I stopped and started treading again panic set in. Passing the five-minute mark, I reluctantly grabbed the pole—again.

Down to my last opportunity, I let go of all fears. I went right to the program director and asked if he could help me. After he cleared the class, we went back to the pool, and he asked me to show him how I treaded water. I got in and showcased my unique style. After a few strokes, he told me to stop, and then he said, "I think I've found your problem. You're doing it all wrong."

"Great, but can you help me fix it?" I pleaded.

Fortunately, the solution was right up my alley since it involved the kick portion of my favorite survival stroke, the elementary backstroke. When he showed me how to integrate the kick with my tread, how to glide and rest between strokes, and then how to finish with controlled breathing, the light came on. I quickly discovered what I needed to do to be successful. I went right to work at it.

I met with him every day, but I also practiced back at my apartment building. I'd wait until midnight, and then I would sneak down to the pool in flight gear and boots. If anyone was there, I'd wait until they got creeped out by me and left. When I was finally alone, I'd work at least an hour on my newfound technique. As the big day approached, I knew it would be a challenge, but I stopped thinking about it. I only thought about technique, rhythm, and controlled breathing.

As I entered the pool for my test, the initial extra buoyancy from precious little air pockets in my flight gear soon gave way to an overly-saturated death trap as my super-cool flight suit and leather boots transformed into an anchor. I continued to think only about technique, rhythm, and controlled breathing. Even with the splashing, labored breathing, and active bamboo pole operations all around me, I continued to focus on technique, rhythm, and controlled breathing. I just kept on working it and working it.

Finally, what seemed like only moments after I started, I felt a tap on my shoulder by one of the bamboo technicians, and I immediately swam away to avoid what I thought was a disqualification trap. Now that he had my attention, he yelled that I was at twenty-two minutes and I could start drown proofing. Wow, the hard part was really over. I did it! I quickly pulled my helmet off and used it for flotation and then immediately focused on technique, rhythm, and controlled breathing for my drown-proofing finale. At the end of thirty minutes, we were allowed to inflate our life preserver and blow air into our g-suit. As I floated on my back, satisfied with my performance and relieved that my career wasn't over before I even sat in a plane, I reflected on what I had learned and how I would approach each new challenge going forward:

★ Hoping for the best is a poor strategy.

★ Worrying and fretting about the worst-case scenario serves no useful purpose.

★ Only when you commit to the moment and focus on what you can control instead of thinking about what you can't control will you be able to move forward and secure your destiny.

☆ The fear of embarrassment or the fear of asking for help is a big
problem. If I had only sought out competent coaching earlier and
put it to good use, I would never have been in that horrible do-or-
die situation in the first place.

Focus on What You Can Control

When it came to getting in the pool, I found that by focusing on the
things I could control—technique, rhythm, and controlled breathing—I
never worried or panicked. It was almost like being in an altered state
of consciousness. What I didn't fully understand and appreciate at the
time was that there was an endless sequence of do-or-die tests in my
future. The swimming challenge was actually a great primer. It led me
to an early system of fear management.

Going through flight school was an endless series of incremental
performance tests, check rides, surprises, and the potential for inflight
emergencies. We memorized procedures and practiced them in simulators. Instructors challenged our judgment and decision-making and really
made us work hard mentally. We constantly reviewed dangerous scenarios in our heads and how we would handle them. We found out all we
could about our instructors so we knew what to expect. Some screamed
at you, some smoked in the cockpit, some liked to pull cockpit circuit
breakers to simulate an emergency, and some would always have their
hands on the controls. I still don't know if I would rather have someone
screaming at me from the back seat or someone who was dead silent.
Needless to say, stress was a persistent part of day-to-day life.

With each new or potential challenge, surprise, or complex situation,
it was drilled into our heads that we needed to chill out. Just like technique, rhythm, and controlled breathing in the pool, the catchphrase

we used in aviation was aviate, navigate, communicate. This forced us to focus on what we could control. That simple but effective technique automatically repressed fear and panic when things start going wrong.

Departing Controlled Flight

Fear or stress induces panic, which forces a physical reaction. In a complex, high-speed environment, the fear reaction often gets you into even more trouble than your original problem. One of the fears in aviation is the dreaded departure from controlled flight. When maneuvering a jet at high angle of attack and high "g," it's not uncommon to go directly from a sleek, high-performance machine to a sleek but falling heap of expensive metal. The jet literally stops flying, and the pilot falls back to earth.

Departures can be extremely violent and disorienting—remember Goose in the movie *Top Gun*? If the aircraft settles into a spin, pilots fully expect to lose 20,000 feet per minute. And if they can "break" the spin, they also know they need at least 5,000 feet to recover. So if they go into a spin at 25,000 feet, they have only a minute to assess, provide proper control inputs, evaluate status, and then pull up and recover before they hit the ground. Given that compressed timeline for survival, what was the first thing we were taught to do during this time-critical emergency? *Wind the clock—obviously.*

Why? It gets back to fear management. The worst thing a pilot can do in a situation like this is to panic and aggravate the situation by moving the control stick in the wrong direction, either prolonging or worsening the departure or spin. Winding the clock is just a metaphor for technique, rhythm, and controlled breathing. It brings pilots back in the moment and allows them to focus on what they can control. It allows them to respond as opposed to reacting.

All aircraft have very specific out-of-control flight procedures. If a pilot puts in the wrong control at the wrong time, he or she can make the situation even worse. In the F/A-18, it was so important to execute the correct procedures at the right time that we would recite them to each other during every tactical mission brief. To this day I can still spew them out, almost eight years after my last tactical flight.

Out-of-Control Flight Procedures

If out of control:

- ❂ Neutralize the stick/feet off rudders/check that your speed brake is in.
- ❂ This is where you would "wind the clock."

If still out of control:

- ❂ Throttles IDLE
- ❂ Altitude, angle of attack, airspeed, yaw rate
- ❂ If recovery indicated, recover

If spin confirmed and command arrow present on the displays:

- ❂ Full lateral stick—with arrow

If spin confirmed and command arrow not present on the displays:

- ❂ Recovery switch—RECOVERY
- ❂ Full lateral stick (left or right) with arrow

When yaw rate stops:

- ❂ Lateral stick smoothly neutral
- ❂ Spin recovery switch—CHECK NORMAL
- ❂ One "g" roll to nearest horizon
- ❂ Throttles—maximum
- ❂ Pull to establish positive rate of climb

(And my favorite)

❂ Passing 6,000 feet with dive recovery not initiated—EJECT

In an out-of-control scenario, not only is the pilot falling at a tremendous rate of speed, but he is also subject to violent and disorienting
thrashing about. As you can see from the long list of procedures, there
are many things to look at and be aware of before a pilot can select the
right response. There is no room for debilitating fear or panic because
it typically produces very bad reactions.

Running Out of Gas

Another big fear in aviation is running out of gas. There is nothing more
embarrassing—except for landing with the landing gear up, I suppose.
This issue is the primary focal point of every operation, especially on an
aircraft carrier where pilots only have one place to land or refuel. Since
flying the F/A-18, I can't remember a single operational flight where
I didn't refuel airborne after I launched. In fighters, "tanking," as it's
called, is like drinking water in the desert—staying hydrated to survive.
If another airplane looked like it had something resembling a basket
with a hose attached to it, F/A-18 pilots would find a way to get fuel
from it. I've tanked from many different aircraft and in many different
environments. I've tanked during the day, at night, in clouds, and at
low altitude. Over time, it became as natural as riding a bike, but it was
pretty intimidating at first.

Think about it. Tanking is the act of inserting a special tube (called
an inflight refueling probe) from a pilot's airplane into the extended
basket of the fuel delivery aircraft, or tanker, while in flight. The pilot is
purposefully ramming another jet. As you can imagine, basket stability

is determined by weather, tanker piloting, and tanker speed and maneuvering. And once the probe is inserted, the pilot must hang out in there
until he gets all the gas he needs, which could take a few minutes. During
the "ramming" phase, I've seen baskets and probes ripped off, baskets
ripping off pieces of the airplane, and pieces of the airplane ingested by
jet motors following a disastrous high-energy miss. Lots of bad things
can happen. Now, throw in the fact that pilots are usually getting gas
because they're in danger of running out of gas. For newer pilots, this
is clearly a situation where they may feel unbridled fear. What does aviation wisdom tell pilots to do to manage fear in this scenario? Wiggle
their toes, of course!

Airborne refueling requires a pilot to be loose and patient. The
pilot has to wait for the basket to stabilize or, if it's moving, he has
to synchronize himself with the movement. Excessive closure speed,
"stabbing" at it, or wild close-in maneuvers that radically reposition
the probe typically don't end well. Fear causes the pilot to tense up
and prevents him from imposing the delicate inputs to the flight controls at the right time. He ends up violently gripping the stick and
throttle—"squeezing the black" out of them, as we say. The act of
simply wiggling their toes creates a mental distraction that relaxes
other parts of the body and allows them to perform. It really is magic.
I guess that's why most relaxation therapists start by having you imagine that your toes are totally relaxed and moving that action up to the
rest of your body from there.

Alone in the Arabian Sea

One night, a colleague of mine once found himself in dire straits due
to no fault of his own. Flying a mission off the USS *Kittyhawk* in the

north Arabian Sea, he returned to the ship to land only to discover that the weather had turned bad, and the ship was making frequent turns to avoid oil platforms. On multiple landing attempts, he was forced to go around as the ship negotiated hazard after hazard. Running low on gas, he requested an Air Force tanker (this is a plane, not a ship, remember). As they approached each other, weather became an even bigger problem. There were no clear areas where they could rendezvous. With less than ten minutes of fuel left, a tricky radar rendezvous and join-up had to be completed—in the clouds. When they finally had sight of each other, the fuel gauge was showing less than 500 pounds (that's five minutes or less before flame-out). With the pilot's toes working overtime, he closed on the tanker, positioned himself behind the basket, and happened to notice the fuel gauge was reading "0" as he engaged (rammed) the basket. Although he successfully got in, he didn't know if he had enough time left for the fuel to pass through his probe, get to the tanks, and then get to the engines. After what seemed like forever, the fuel gauge started moving off "0." Thankfully, he was still flying. For his efforts, including a lot of clock winding and toe wiggling, he earned an air medal, a decoration for extraordinary airmanship.

Combat: When Your First Priority Is Not Yourself

Winding the clock and wiggling your toes are part of many routine Navy aviation stories where fear needs to be choked down and muted in order to perform at the highest level. But what about combat? Before my very first combat mission, I wondered how I would eventually perform. Would I choke? Would I survive? Would I screw up? I spent a lot of time talking to Viet Nam-era pilots about their experiences. It was interesting to me that some of the people they thought would do great things didn't do so well, and some of the people they thought would perform horribly became notable heroes. Having had the benefit of serving with the Naval Strike and Air Warfare Center (now called the Naval Aviation Warfighting Development Center and home of Top Gun), I heard the accounts of some of the most celebrated fighter pilots in US history during our "MiG Killer Debrief" series. The term "MiG" is short for the Russian company that manufactured Russian fighter aircraft, and it has become synonymous with enemy aircraft. I noticed during these sessions that a theme started to emerge.

All the stories I heard described the culture and environment during each respective "MiG killer's" time period. The pilots talked about the political environment, the aircraft they flew, and the missions they were part of. They shared the lessons they learned as they matured in combat. Eventually they got to the juicy part—the "shoot down." Without fail, the strongest motivation was to help a wingman, support a friendly aircraft, or cover a ground unit in distress. This unwritten contract and sense of duty seemed to move these legends to ignore their own personal safety and take on extra risk in order to help out. Fear just seemed to evaporate. When asked about it, the common reply was, "Sure, I was scared, but there was no one else to do it." These amazing people didn't consider themselves heroes. To them it was just preparation meeting opportunity meeting fear suppression. They did what was needed because no one else could.

The pure motivation to help others who are defenseless and to complete one's mission make for very powerful fear neutralizers. To me, it is no different from a mother protecting her child or someone pulling a stranger from a burning building or car. In thinking back, there is nothing I wouldn't have done to protect and support my wingman or my flight. In that regard, even with all the other fear management tools working, I don't think it is possible to fully manage fear when your first priority is yourself.

Containing Your Fear: Willy Driscoll

As part of our Top Gun training, we spent a whole day talking about managing fear (we call it *combat stress* to make it sound tougher, I guess). For years, one of naval aviation's legends, Willy Driscoll, would share his own experience with stress and fear management. Willy was a radar intercept officer. He and Duke Cunningham, his pilot, used their trusty F-4 Phantom II to become the Navy's only Viet Nam War aces. Willy flew 170 combat missions, and three of his five kills occurred on the same day. We were all in awe of him. He is now a renowned speaker who focuses on peak performance under pressure.

The first time I saw his presentation, I was a little surprised by all the different-sized household liquid containers he had lined up. Set out next to each other in increasing size were vials, bottles, and jugs. I couldn't imagine what they were for.

He pulled out the smallest container first and explained that the liquid in the container represented stress, fear, and anxiety. He likened this first small medicine vial of stress on the same scale as going out on a pilot's first check ride. Everyone immediately had a reference point. The next container was about the size of a water bottle. The stress level related to it, he said, was landing on an aircraft carrier at night for the first time. Again, we could all relate. He then went on to a major aircraft emergency; the representative bottle was about the size of a 7-Eleven Big Gulp. Most of us could still relate. Then he got to the big containers and what they stood for. At this point we could only take his word for it.

He told us the gallon jug represented getting shot at for the first

continued

time. This was, for most of us, uncharted territory, so our attention level immediately picked up. He recalled having to evade multiple surface-to-air missiles tracking his jet. He calmly mentioned that as long as you saw them, it wasn't a big deal. And what if you didn't see them?

At the end of the presentation, he brought out a monstrous jug like the big ones used in a water cooler. This was the getting-hit-by-a-missile stress jug.

As Willy's story went, he had just finishing shooting down his third, fourth, and fifth enemy aircraft on May 10, 1972—yes, three at once. On the way back to the ship, his jet was hit by a surface-to-air missile. Still over land, the crew nursed the wounded jet along, and by managing multiple cockpit emergencies (such as both hydraulic systems failing) in a composed and competent fashion, they improved their chances of rescue by getting closer and closer to the ocean. I'm sure the containers for "ejection over enemy territory" and "prisoner of war" wouldn't have fit into the room.

As a result of their great work and composure, when the jet finally quit and started falling from the sky, Willy and Duke had actually made it to the coastline, but they were still very close to hostile territory. During the ride down, they recognized enemy boats and took out their handguns just in case. Feeling exposed coming down in their parachutes, they were relieved to finally hit the water and began treading as they managed to inflate their life rafts and vests. (I thought to myself, *I guess that swimming training I complained about is really important after all*.) Once safe from the water hazard, they immediately tried to separate as far as possible from the enemy. With air cover and a helicopter nearby, they were eventually picked up and returned to their ship, none the worse for wear.

Willy's liquid stress containers presented the perfect visual prop for showing the importance of countering stress with an equal magnitude stress management method.

Fear, Stress, and Anxiety Need to Be Contained

The containers in Willy's presentation are very symbolic. Fear, stress, and anxiety need to be contained. The bigger the stress, the bigger the container you need to accommodate it. The size of your own personal container is determined by a few simple things:

★ your preparation and your experience

★ your faith

★ your ability to stay in the moment and focus on what you *can* do and *can* control rather than what you *can't* do

★ having a contract with others that places you secondary to them and your mission

★ understanding the difference between reacting and responding

Reaction Versus Response

You hear it all the time in sports—"great reaction time." The ability to sense, orient, and act are crucial factors when it comes to any performance measure. In my mind, though, reaction is purely the time it takes to produce a behavior, starting from the moment you're stimulated by something. There is nothing that states that the behavior has to be useful, valuable, or rewarding.

A response, on the other hand, involves selecting the best of several options—including doing absolutely nothing—following an event that requires your action. Professional baseball players don't merely react when the ball is pitched. They evaluate all the cues . . . the release, the speed, the trajectory . . . and then they recalibrate their swing, step back, or duck. The great hitters choose from multiple responses, and this all happens in approximately four-tenths of a second. In the pros, players need to swing their bat when the ball is twenty to thirty feet from them. How to do they do it?

Nerve signals travel at about 250 miles per hour. All the necessary decision-making information can be acquired in forty-three-thousandths of a second. Then processing begins. Experienced hitters can decide and move on to muscle coordination pretty quickly. Conversely, an inexperienced hitter has to battle with processing delays that usually conclude with the wrong or no action. Even the best hitters still only have a 30 percent chance of getting a hit that puts them on base. But they are responding versus reacting.

Sometimes in a fighter cockpit, things happen at similar speeds, but usually they don't. And although fighter pilots spend lots of time perfecting their responses by rigorously training to sight cues and other complementary information, the adverse combination of fear, stress, or inexperience can often disrupt or undermine the process. When fear or stress is present and uncontained, each pilot has a dominant "go-to" reaction that occludes all other behaviors, such as pulling up and adding full power. The equivalent in a car is probably hard braking. Not a bad go-to move, but it is rarely the best option.

This is where the winding the clock strategy can help us select the best option. With kids, as with baseball players and fighter pilots, controlled failure training, developing disciplined responses to certain unambiguous cues (an out-of-control flight, for example), and focusing on the moment help mute performance fears and increase optimal responses. When decision-making speeds reach baseball hitting standards, I suspect that even the best fighter pilots select the perfect optimal action only 30 percent of the time as well. The good news is that you are always improving your probability of success.

What about surprises and unique situations? What if you encounter something you have never experienced or prepared for? Good questions, but I harken back to the construction of your stress (fear) container. If you can stay in the moment, work on what you can control and influence, and respond rather than react, eventually you get ahead of the threat, no matter what it is.

After 9/11

As a naval installation commander, I once had the good fortune to spend an informal afternoon with former New York City Mayor Rudy Giuliani and a small group of military commanders. It was 2005, so the 9/11 attacks were still pretty recent and the repercussions were still being felt in every part of our lives. Our small group of military commanders was very interested in how Giuliani responded to the attack and made decisions amid the chaos and confusion. From our perspective, his grasp of the situation, his leadership, and the actions he took not only minimized the damage and kept the city functioning, but also comforted an entire nation.

Eventually he was asked if the city had ever contemplated a situation where a large jet would be used as a weapon and if they had prepared for it in any meaningful way. Mayor Giuliani thought for a second, and then answered both yes and no. He went on to explain that the World Trade Center had been attacked before with nearly the same horrendous results. Although the tower didn't collapse and fall into the adjacent tower as planned in that earlier attack, six people died and over a thousand were injured. And if the truck and bomb had been parked closer to the tower's structural components, the terrorists may very well have been successful.

He then went on to detail the kind of situations they had been preparing for. First, they thought it was imperative to have optimal command

and control. As a result, they had built alternate emergency HQ sites in case the primary HQ was destroyed or unusable. These alternate sites were routinely exercised. They invested in sustainable and redundant communications, and they made sure they could control all of New York City's public safety assets. Next, they became experts at large building evacuations. With so many skyscrapers, they realized this was an important public safety function they had to be good at. And the final key scenario they had been preparing for was a mass casualty event. In so doing, they had a system in place that could evaluate hospital loading, recall emergency medical professionals, and optimize on-scene medical support and transportation. Giuliani credited the preparation in all these areas as important factors in responding rather than reacting to the 9/11 crisis.

By activating the alternate emergency HQs, they were able to organize their resources, integrate pieces of multiple indirect plans, and deploy their assets in the most productive way. Because of an aggressive evacuation plan and optimal use of medical resources, many more people survived the attack than would have otherwise. Recovery efforts were also streamlined, and outside assistance was quickly integrated into the effort. During all of this, Mayor Giuliani added that they were still very concerned with potential follow-on attacks.

We didn't ask if he was scared, but I'm sure he would have said yes. He clearly managed his fear the same way fighter pilots do. He worked in the moment. He focused on what he could control and influence. He put the safety and needs of others ahead of himself. He "wound the clock" at the right times, and he "wiggled his toes" when he needed to. And most importantly, when faced with a huge, catastrophic, unanticipated surprise, he responded instead of reacting, blending his city's capabilities in creative and timely ways. It goes without saying that he definitely had one of the largest stress containers in Willy Driscoll's presentation.

A note of caution, though: Managing persistent high-volume fear or stress can take a toll. Over time, it drains you and can negatively affect your health. I'll never forget a set of time-sequenced pictures I saw of a famous World War II German fighter pilot. During one of our training lectures, a picture of a youthful Erich "Bubi" Hartmann, the most successful fighter pilot in air warfare history, was presented, accompanied by a list of his amazing aviation feats. With 352 kills to his credit, this German ace earned the nickname the "Black Devil" from his Russian adversaries. His differentiating talents included "keen eyesight, lightning reflexes, an aggressive spirit, and the ability to stay cool in combat."

His first kill was in November 1943 at the age of twenty-one. His last kill was in March 1945. At the end of the war, instead of flying his plane to the British sector and relative safety, he stayed behind with his squadron and their families, where he was taken prisoner by the Russians in May 1945. Just before he was captured, another picture was taken. When compared to the first picture, just prior to his first kill, he was nearly unrecognizable. In the span of less than two years he looked as though he had aged twenty years. Acute stress, anxiety, and fear is not friendly to the body over a long period of time.

The physical response to fear, even if managed properly, can be intense. Heart rate increases, blood pumps to muscles, eyesight sharpens, and hormones flow to the brain to aid in focusing. Living under constant fear or stress weakens the immune system, can cause cardiovascular damage, and can produce gastrointestinal problems. As effective as fear management techniques can be in the presence of acute stress, the physiological sequence is still activated and can cause damage. With Erich Hartmann, fear and stress were clearly manifested in his physical appearance. In addition, original stress can create a memory marker that can trigger the same physiological effects simply by recalling the event anytime in the future. The gift that keeps on giving, so to speak.

So added to fear management techniques that help counter the immediate physical changes brought on by fear and stress, you also need to account for fatigue, fitness, and health. Without rest, adequate health, and fitness, the ability to battle a prolonged barrage of high stress or fear can be significantly compromised. In most situations, stress is typically not a one-and-done proposition. It usually involves multiple or evolving stress contributors that can wear you down physically and mentally over time. In order to build up the necessary and important reserves to sustain you through prolonged stress, a premium must be paid in the areas of rest, nutrition, and exercise. Unfortunately, these are the very things that most people tend to sacrifice first when faced with imminent or persistent stress, anxiety, and fear.

Stress Management: Pilots and Children

The prescriptions for fear and stress management I've offered so far, although imperative for fighter pilots performing at a high level, can be equally beneficial to the normal, average kid. The range of perceived high stress and fear events our youth face is endless. It could be anything: finals, auditions, public speaking, the big game, prom, or even dressing for school. Stress and fear are clearly in the eye of the beholder. Everyone processes stress and fear in different ways. There are many fighter pilots who would rather be shot at then to have to dance publicly (don't judge). But there is one fear that deserves special attention, one I spend a lot of time on with my own kids: the fear of failure.

"The fear of failure is the most insidious fear of all. Why? Because it always seems to be the root cause of never trying."

The fear of failure is the most insidious

fear of all. Why? Because it always seems to be the root cause of never trying. Nobody wants to be embarrassed. Nobody wants to disappoint anyone. Nobody wants to get the blame. Nobody wants to fail. This fear alone has prevented many gifted and talented people from following their passion and doing what they love—or at least seeing how far they could take it.

We've all seen people crumble when the expectations placed upon them get higher. There are many names for this, but choking is the predominant one. This singular fear has fascinated me ever since my trepidations of flying in combat for the first time. Would I perform? Would I successfully complete my mission? Would I return? Would I serve with honor as a prisoner of war? Honestly, you'll never know until you get there, so I eventually determined that it wasn't in my best interest to dwell or obsess over it. Of course, this is much harder to do than say.

Teaching Students to Land

When I started teaching students to land on the ship for the first time, I also started noticing a peculiar trend. Like clockwork, the same demographic breakdown would present itself with each class. There was always a small group that displayed exceptional performance throughout the entire training phase. They knew their emergency procedures cold. They exceled in their simulators and field landings. And when they went out to the ship, they were equally impressive there.

In contrast to this group, the next group was exceptionally slow. They always needed extra instruction, extra simulators, and extra field landings. In this group, there were some that weren't even allowed to go to the ship with the rest of their class because of the perceived safety risk. And of the students from this group that we ultimately took to the ship, most either were disqualified or just barely qualified.

I considered myself to be part of the third, or "normal," group. My group had lots of ups and downs. We had some good days and some bad days. At some point we experienced an aha moment and generally finished strong just before we flew out to the ship. While at the ship, we were generally solid, and some of us actually outperformed everyone else.

The fourth and final group performed above average. It was as if they had been doing precision landings their entire lives. Their deviations were minimal, and their corrections were finely calibrated. They were so good that struggling students from the other groups would often go to them for guidance; they seemed to have this whole carrier landing thing wired. Over time though, this was the group that concerned me most.

It never failed that one or two from this elite group would underperform—some horribly so. You see, no matter how hard we strived to re-create the ship landing environment at the field and in simulators, the real ship was very, very different. For most of the pilots, it was the first time they couldn't see land. At night, under the clouds, it was as dark as they had ever experienced. Landing technique was different as well. They usually had to carry a little more power because the winds were higher. They were also required to make quite a few more heading changes due to the eight-degree misalignment between the ship's heading and the actual landing direction. Oh, and sometimes the ship even moved a little.

For a pilot that had been in the "zone" at the field, this new environment was a shock to the system. No longer was he or she the master. The deviations and the required corrections were much more pronounced than anything they had ever experienced. When expecting to have the same performance and success as they did at the field, their new reality truly shook their confidence.

I found it very interesting that the most confident and proven performers could be so easily shaken when things didn't go exactly the way they expected. For the very first time, failure, in their minds, was now a very likely possibility. And when this fear of failure started to dominate their thoughts, it was very difficult to get them back in the moment and back to the abundant skills they already possessed. They forgot that they had everything they needed to get the job done.

I made it a special point to prepare this particular group mentally for the likelihood of potential setbacks. Aside from operating in the moment and focusing on their own sphere of influence and control, they also needed a system that would help them deal with unanticipated adversity. By acknowledging the possibility of things going wrong and having contingency options to fall back on, they were more likely to focus on the moment and gracefully deploy their skills in an effective way when their situation frequently changed.

To prevent my kids from being victimized by their own fear of failure, I've found that I had to prepare them in the same way we prepare fighter pilots. It is when preparation meets opportunity and opportunity meets fear management that they can step forward, perform, and either achieve success or live to fight another day.

FIGHTER PILOT PARENT TAKEAWAYS—
Managing Fear Principles

☆ Teach your children that most fear is irrational: "I don't test well, therefore, I won't do well on the test."

☆ A rational (and therefore acceptable) fear pairs a realistic performance expectation with a realistic capability mismatch: "We didn't go over that in class, but we are being tested on it."

☆ Show children how to address a rational fear by taking a useful action immediately: "I will see my teacher, review the study guide for that section, or watch YouTube videos from other teachers."

☆ Show children how to "chill out," "wind the clock," and "wiggle your toes." When they relax, their preparation and problem-solving capability will rise to the surface.

☆ Show children how to *respond* instead of *react* through conditioning (controlled failure). When times get tough, there is no greater feeling for them than to recognize that "I've been here before."

☆ Stress staying in the moment and focusing on what they can control in the here and now. It's the only place they can make a difference and drive positive outcomes.

☆ Show them how to put others first. There is something magical about mastering fear when you place others ahead of yourself.

☆ Don't cause kids to burn out through excessive stress and fear management. Make sure they get plenty of breaks and can recover between stress events.

CHAPTER EIGHT

RECOGNITION, REWARDS, AND CELEBRATIONS

Humans need recognition. We crave it. We work for it. We are proud of it. We tell our family and friends about it. We relive recognition moments over and over in our minds as we enjoy remembering the emotional high we experienced. But one caveat about recognition and rewards is that for them to be meaningful they must be deserved, and they must be scaled to the achievement.

If they are not, they can become a source of embarrassment, resentment, and—ironically—they can lower performance, which is the exact opposite of what recognition and rewards are supposed to inspire. And unlike economic inflation, recognition inflation is almost impossible to recalibrate. It can be a powerful motivator, but increasingly it seems to be a source of reduced standards and lower expectations. Everybody likes medals. Right?

How to Inspire Your Troops

During the Revolutionary War, our first president was frustrated with the lack of support Congress was providing to his military. His men went without pay and supplies while simultaneously being asked to suffer extreme hardships and make extraordinary sacrifices. It was not an easy life, and Washington recognized that the situation required every tool he could find to inspire his beloved troops to persevere.

To make matters worse, the typical recognition tool of the day—field commissions—was also taken away. With seemingly nothing left for him to use to recognize and foster meritorious service, gallantry, and fidelity, he created the very first US military awards—the Badge of Distinction and the Badge of Military Merit. The Badge of Military Merit was the prototype for the Medal of Honor and was similar in appearance to the Purple Heart. But with the end of the war close at hand, Washington was surprised and disappointed to learn that there had been no recommendations for either of these awards. This was a ground zero moment for the US military. Washington was so incensed that he ordered a review board to be assembled and awards to be presented before the Continental Army was due to be disbanded.

Despite eight years of war against a very powerful adversary, a war in which the Continental Army defied all odds in pursuit of victory, the review board only identified three candidates: Sergeant Elijah Churchill, Fourth Troop, Second Troop of Light Dragoons; Sergeant William Brown of the 5th Connecticut Regiment; and Sergeant Daniel Bissell of the 2nd Connecticut Regiment, a spy who had been embedded with Benedict Arnold's loyalists. Only *three*. And there wasn't a single military medal, badge, or award issued for another seventy-eight years until the Medal of Honor was created in 1861. That's when recognition inflation started to kick in.

By the end of the Civil War, 1,520 Medals of Honor had been awarded to those who "most distinguished themselves by their gallantry in action, and other soldier-like qualities."[4] By 1871, so many were receiving the award that a new condition was added: "The conduct which deserves such recognition should not be the simple discharge of duty, but such acts beyond this that if omitted or refused to be done, should not justly subject the person to censure as a shortcoming or failure."[5] In other words, it required more than just showing up.

It got worse. By 1897, President William McKinley had to refine the criteria even further by including "gallantry and intrepidity above and beyond that of one's fellow soldiers"[6] as a discriminating condition. This was a direct response to the recognition inflation observed when over 900 Civil War soldiers petitioned for medals nearly twenty-five years after the war was over. The medal issue became such a source of resentment and embarrassment that in 1917 a review panel was established. The panel eventually struck down a total of 911 medals that had been previously awarded.

Given this correction, at present, just over 3,500 Medal of Honor awards have been conferred. Having read most of the more recent citations, the accounts of each celebrated action are truly riveting and inspiring. Sadly, many of the citations end by noting the death of the recipient. Posthumous presentations to families are not uncommon.

The Medal of Honor is now the most revered, respected, and highest award for valor in the US military, an honor that very few will ever earn and none can ever prepare for. In this unique recognition case, the value and integrity of our very first medal has been restored; however, military recognition inflation has found alternate paths.

4, 5, 6 Congressional Medal of Honor Society, http://www.cmohs.org/medal-history.php

Following Washington's 3 Revolutionary War Badge of Merit awards, and Lincoln's 1,520 Civil War Medal of Honor awards, an additional 151 different medals and ribbons have since been created. Of these new awards, the lowest precedent medals are the Navy and Coast Guard Pistol Marksmanship Medals. I was even surprised to see that the Prisoner of War Medal, a medal for someone who was captured and subjected to torture and harsh conditions, is just one step higher than a Good Conduct Medal, a medal that is automatically issued after three years of *honorable and faithful* service. Translated, it means that a recipient basically stayed out of trouble for three years. In my opinion, probably 40 percent of these newer recognition tools fail to deliver on their objective—which should be inspiration and improved performance.

The defining moment in clarifying my understanding and approach to recognition occurred early in my career at a recognition event. It is very typical for squadrons to assemble weekly for what they call "Quarters." At Quarters, the whole squadron meets so the commanding officer can communicate critical information, address concerns, and answer questions. It's also the primary platform for recognition and advancement. Family and friends are invited to observe or participate, photographers capture the moment up close, and there is usually an accompanying story in the base newspaper. All good . . . so far.

At this particular Quarters, which was held in a hangar, the awardees arrived early in formal dress and then lined up according to their award precedent. Lower awards were presented first, and the best were saved for last. In this group, there was a highly regarded pilot who had just joined our shore-based training squadron after three years of flying the A-7 Corsair II. He had two deployments, combat operations, and lots of day and night traps under his belt—arduous, challenging, and dangerous work by any standard. The students were eager to learn from him, and his new instructor peers were glad to leverage his recent combat experience to enhance the training curriculum. His would be the one citation everyone would pay close attention to.

As the rest of the squadron assembled behind the awardees, and the entire group of 250 people organized themselves in precise ranks, the absence of movement signaled that the show was about to begin. Right on the dot, the executive officer (XO) brought the squadron to attention, which cued the commanding officer (CO). He entered the hangar and went up to the first person in the awardee line. Someone would read the award citation over the public announcement system while the CO pinned the medal on the recipient. While waiting for what I considered the "headliner" citation, I listened to descriptions of the others. A small group of awardees were all receiving the same medal, so I was curious to hear what they had each done to earn it. In my mind, it was a pretty big deal, so I was expecting some pretty impressive actions, but that wasn't the case to my surprise.

Then they finally got to the last awardee—the A-7 pilot. As expected, the accomplishments in his citation were impressive. As I listened intently to the conclusion, I finally realized that he was receiving the same medal, a Navy Achievement Medal, as the three awardees who preceded him. I started to think that the person reading the citation was out of sequence with the CO or had misread it. But no, the medal was affixed to the pilot's chest, and the CO stepped away. The pilot had received the same award as the others, but for significantly different reasons.

What *really* got me was that one officer received the same medal as the A-7 pilot for having ordered portable toilets for the squadron open house! I couldn't help but feel embarrassed for the combat veteran who received the same medal as the Porta-Potty king. I could sense the discomfort the CO was feeling for his role in signing such frivolous and inflated awards. I also felt sorry for the people that received them. They took no pride or sense of achievement in what they were being recognized for—they were clearly embarrassed. It was obvious that there was a huge disparity in how recognition was allocated, and in this case, it served only to compromise truly extraordinary achievement.

> "I understood that recognition was an important tool to help incentivize certain behaviors, but I also discovered firsthand that it is fraught with danger."

This was a critical moment in my view of recognition and rewards. I understood that recognition was an important tool to help incentivize certain behaviors, but I also discovered firsthand that it is fraught with danger. At that moment, I personally committed to getting it right and being consistent whenever I had the honor, privilege, and sacred duty of recognizing superior performance and achievement in the future. This commitment would eventually carry into parenthood for me.

The Dark Side of Recognition

Clearly, subjective recognition has a dark side. What about purely objective recognition? Are there dangers there too? No one can argue with "the numbers," can they? You can eliminate all controversy and suspicion, can't you? It makes recognition simple and easy, right? No, not so fast. There are problems here as well.

Once a recognition standard is established and exceeded, the incentive to try harder or dream bigger for those who have already achieved the standard is corrupted. The only recourse, then, is to continually change the number. Otherwise, what's left is a system of perpetual mediocrity where recognition supersedes growth and higher achievement.

Objective recognition demands proper context to be useful. With kids, since they change so fast and have the potential to achieve so much in such short durations, objective metrics become obsolete very quickly. If you don't frequently update the number, whenever the current number is no longer a challenge, you then run the risk of stunting their graduation to the next level. For their sake, keep the number current and achievable. From setting a recognition goal for how high one child can count to how many times another can jump rope, keep changing the number in achievable chunks.

There is one other problem with objective-based recognition worth mentioning: unintended consequences. It is not uncommon for recognition seekers to pad their resume or focus on a very narrow part of their job or responsibilities in order to earn the recognition they desire. When this happens, it can undermine the reward process and become counterproductive for both themselves and their teams. Although difficult to prove, I have seen situations where squadrons seemed to deny training opportunities to more junior pilots for fear they would hurt the greenie board in the last few days of a landing competition.

> "With kids, since they change so fast and have the potential to achieve so much in such short durations, objective metrics become obsolete very quickly."

Sometimes, especially with parents, it happens very innocently. For example, the mom who offers her son ten dollars for each goal he scores in soccer may have just changed the outcome of a game, as well as her son's future play time if he ends up becoming selfish and starts making poor decisions when playing. This is where statistics and objective recognition start to falter. The specific (goals scored) starts to undermine the ultimate objective (games won and quality play time).

When it became my turn to award medals, I discovered that it was a lot harder than it looks. I finally and begrudgingly had to accept the fact that sometimes the wrong people get recognized for the wrong reasons, and the true heroes are sometimes left in the shadows. But despite the occasional unfairness of it all, eventually the most deserving earn something much more significant: trust and respect within their teams.

The issue of the wrong people getting recognized for the wrong reasons is really tough for some parents. How is a child to develop self-esteem, confidence, and passion for something if they aren't constantly rewarded for an action or behavior, no matter how slight or insignificant? The lesson that I reinforce with my kids is that there is no better reward than the satisfaction of having worked hard and having completed or mastered a relatively tough task, independent of age, complexity, or the time it takes to complete. The reward is immediate, and the people you respect the most will already know and celebrate with you. Whether or not you receive credit or formal recognition doesn't really matter if you keep your personal accounting of achievement in good order. The recognition that I cherish the most was the slap on the back and a genuine "Great job!" from someone I respected and held in high regard. Having worked in the top-secret world for so long, it was usually best that nobody knew about what we did anyhow.

"Ultimately, children will understand that they are being recognized for something far more important—their character and integrity."

It's clear that the moment you start doing things simply for recognition, you are doing them for the wrong reason. Sure, it is great and wonderful to be recognized publicly, but don't expect it—and by all means don't promote yourself. It is the quickest path to permanent loss of credibility and respect. And if someone else gets the credit, you should congratulate them and move on.

It should go without saying, but the next big lesson I share with my kids is that if you are disproportionately recognized for any achievement, set the record straight and give credit to those who deserve it. Show your humility and honesty instead. Every great leader I've ever experienced immediately diverts recognition to their team. Ultimately, children will understand that they are being recognized for something far more important—their character and integrity. That type of recognition carries the ultimate cachet.

I am always intrigued when political "leaders" describe their accomplishments and discriminating attributes. I understand the political environment they operate in, but as soon as I see them claiming personal responsibility for an achievement, or embellishing or exaggerating something that happened on their watch, their credibility is permanently damaged with me. Conversely, when they divert positive recognition to their staff while accepting blame for failures, their credibility, as well as their likability, go way up. The best teams I've had the fortune to be part of are decisively the ones that are solutions- and results-focused, not recognition-focused. Imagine how different society would work if no one cared who got the credit as long as there was a win at the end.

Standing on the Shoulders of Giants

With my nearly 1,000 aircraft carrier landings (a good percentage of them at night), it became clear to me that my landing performance was only partially attributable to my skill and ability. In reality, I had the good fortune to have a whole team behind me helping to make me look respectable. Sometimes, though, even they couldn't pull it off.

Imagine driving a car that hasn't been tuned up, tends to pull to the left, has a headlight out, and only plays AM radio. How well do you think you would drive in bad weather, low visibility, challenging roads, or dense traffic? Not that easily, right? Well, aircraft are similar in a sense, except you don't have the option to pull over. Without meticulously groomed landing systems and the enhanced confidence that goes with them, exemplary performance at the back of the ship is significantly more challenging. In fact, whenever I saw a squadron performing at a high level, I automatically assumed they had a great maintenance program. It would be rare for pilots who enjoyed exceptionally maintained aircraft not to also enjoy exceptional landing performance. But did maintenance ever get the credit they deserve? The really good squadrons definitely make a point of recognizing maintenance personnel. It doesn't stop with maintenance, though.

In carrier aviation, the best landing environment occurs when the ship is aligned with the winds and seas. And as hard as it is for an aviator to give credit to a ship driver for his landing success, their critical seamanship skills, especially in adverse weather conditions, can make a huge difference. Having the right team on the bridge can often be the deciding factor in getting all aircraft aboard quickly. Does the officer of the deck (OOD) and his team ever receive the credit they deserve? Probably nowhere near as much as they should. But they are still heroes in my book.

I could go on and on about the approach controllers, the flight deck crew, the landing signal officers, the representatives in the tower, and yes, even the chaplains, but the simple point is: They all make a critical contribution to success. They are clearly worthy of recognition, but they rarely get it. Do they care? Is recognition a priority for them? I doubt it, but that is probably only because, instead of public praise and acknowledgment, they are rewarded with the truest and most sincere form of recognition: trust and respect. To me, that is the highest form of recognition. But the really, really good pilots—the kind I want my kids to emulate—try to find the time to thank and commend each person who contributes to their success—especially on those very dark and scary nights where safety margins are razor-thin.

More Powerful than Medals

In all honesty, trust and respect are more powerful than medals, citations, newspaper articles, trophies, and even ice cream (when you get older). Trust and respect are tough to earn and easy to lose. But when you are trusted and you enjoy the respect of others, you are more inclined to live up to that trust and perform at a much higher level, which earns you even greater trust and respect. This is the cycle we discussed previously that allows ordinary people to do extraordinary things. My daughters have seen it on the soccer field where play time is directly correlated to how much the coach trusts the players to perform and stick to the game plan. That trust was developed over time in practice and in game situations. This concept is essential for kids to understand and experience. It took on a whole new meaning for me when I had the opportunity to talk to former Soviet Union pilots and the commanding officer of one of India's aircraft carriers, the INS *Viraat*.

I think I can even make a convincing argument as to why trust and respect—or rather, their opposite, suspicion and contempt—may have even led to the end of the Cold War.

Until she was decommissioned in 2017, the INS *Viraat* was considered the oldest aircraft carrier in the world still in service. Originally named the HMS *Hermes*, she had the distinction of participating in the 1982 Falkland Islands Campaign as the Royal Navy's flagship. After being in service for nearly thirty years, she was being replaced by a newer Russian-designed aircraft carrier. But based on her historical value alone, she was definitely worth a walk-through while she was still active.

So, during an official visit to Mumbai as chief of mission for the US Armed Forces Triathlon Team, I took the opportunity to visit the *Viraat*. The chief of mission job sounds much more official, exciting, and glamorous than it is. My main function was to go to formal receptions and dinners with other senior military officers from around the globe, in the spirit of peace and fellowship. Meanwhile, our respective teams were competing in something similar to the Olympics. Through my growing dinner and reception network, I finally found the right person to advance my informal request to tour the *Viraat*.

Eventually, and perhaps as an acknowledgment of my superior dinner and reception skills, I was approached by a senior Indian naval officer who told me that my request had been approved—but that I could only go alone. I thought it was pretty cool for a fighter pilot to board a combatant ship he had flown over years earlier, albeit accidently, nearly causing an international incident. Despite the friendly relationship with India, when we operate armed jets near their fleet without approval or communication, it is still considered threatening.

On tour day, I put on my "whites" (my formal uniform) and waited in the oppressive heat and humidity for the car and driver they sent. Driving in India is not for the faint of heart. Truth be told, in Mumbai the car horn is probably the most important and most often used safety device on the streets. If you're driving, going anywhere without one is a suicide mission. I was relieved to finally arrive at the gate and leave the multiple near-death experiences behind me. As we entered the Indian naval base, I couldn't help but recall the countless hours of threat recognition training I received at the height of the Cold War. The Indians had been frequent buyers of Soviet armament, especially for their army and navy, and they also had a smattering of ships from other countries. As I tried to recall the mnemonics we recited to unleash all the intricate details of the ships we passed, the INS *Viraat* grew visible in the background. At the pier, I was immediately met by one of the ship's more senior officers.

For the most part, ships are ships, and the Indians, like Americans, take nearly all of their official naval protocols from the British. I was, therefore, on automatic pilot as I walked up the gangplank, rendered a salute, requested permission to board, and stepped onto the *Viraat*. My initial reaction was similar to walking through a museum: It looked to me like everything was old and obsolete. The sailor who was serving as my tour guide, although extremely professional and charismatic, was very aggressive with the pace of the tour. This surprised me, because most sailors, independent of the country they serve, reflect pride for their ship and shipmates by wrenching out every detail and sharing every piece of insider trivia when they present their ship. This sailor also kept looking at his watch. I finally asked tactfully if I was keeping him from something, to which he responded, sounding almost embarrassed, "The captain is waiting for you in his cabin." So as not to be rude, I waived the rest of the tour and encouraged him to take me there directly. This is where the recognition value of trust and respect really overpowered me.

As I entered the CO's cabin, with the intent of really drilling down on the specifics of Indian naval strategy and professional ship life, I could sense my plan was being quickly shelved. Almost immediately after the normal and expected professional honors and platitudes, the discussion took a sharp and permanent turn toward US aircraft carriers and aviation. At that time, the Indians were aggressively pursuing a major shift in their naval doctrine, which included the adaptation of Russian-designed aircraft carriers, complete with catapults and arresting gear, similar to US carriers—something they had never done before. I'm sure the prospect of migrating to something so radically different from their history of flight operations conducted by jets designed to take off and land independently of ship systems was intimidating, and thus it was central in their thoughts and concerns. It took the US years to master such a complex mission.

They were doing all the right things, though. As they were awaiting their Russian aircraft, they began sending pilots to train with the US Navy. In fact, our Indian liaison officer was a future MiG-29 pilot who had been trained to land on US aircraft carriers. As I would soon find out, there was a much more serious concern facing the *Viraat*'s commander. "How do you train the enlisted personnel who work on the flight deck?" he asked me.

His question was not uncommon. Amid the noise, power, excitement, and thrill of watching flight operations, every visitor—without exception—always cites with amazement the extraordinary professionalism and artistry of the eighteen-year-olds who

"How is it possible? How do you get them to do that?"

manage flight deck operations. "How is it possible? How do you get them to do that?"

As I do with most people who ask, I went through my crawl-walk-run approach and my controlled failure techniques. The commander wasn't satisfied. I then went into detail about classroom training and how they have to demonstrate and validate their critical skill attainment. He still was not satisfied. I took him through a variety of flight operations scenarios, including key roles and critical tasks, and I described how safety was managed. Finally fascinated, he drilled down and took notes. When I got to the catapult launch sequence, he looked at me in disbelief. *What had I just said that seemed so incomprehensible to him?*

Playing off his body language, I went back to the part where I was explaining all the things that need to happen when an aircraft is taxied to the catapult. I started with the part where the jet, as it approaches the catapult hookup, is bracketed by several young technicians who are looking for any abnormalities with either the aircraft or the catapult. So far so good. I then talked through the steps required to connect the aircraft launch bar to the catapult shuttle. Still good. I explained how dangerous the next phase was—when the aircraft comes up to full power and the pilot cycles the flight controls and checks the instruments. (Although very infrequent, some young and maybe inexperienced technicians have been sucked into the jet's intake or chopped up by a propeller during this phase.) When pilots are satisfied that all cockpit checks are complete, they communicate their "good to go" status by saluting the catapult officer or turning their lights on if it's night.

"And then the aircraft is launched?" the commander asked.

"No, not quite," I answered. I went on to explain that the two most critical safety checks are also happening simultaneously.

The first involves the two young enlisted technicians who are meticulously looking at the aircraft. And the second involves the two young enlisted technicians who are meticulously looking at the catapult systems. As I described what each one does and how important they were, I could sense I was very close to the point where I had lost him earlier. Just after I finished saying, "And any one of these young enlisted technicians can stop the launch if they are not satisfied," he stopped me to clarify.

"So you are saying that an enlisted man can tell a pilot that they can't launch their own aircraft?"

"Yes, that is correct," I replied.

Scowling, he observed, "Well, that will never happen in India."

Why not? It's simple: trust and respect.

Although the Indian caste system is officially gone, the social, economic, and educational gap that divides and separates enlisted ranks from officers still remains. Indian officers typically look down on their enlisted personnel, which has serious trust and respect implications. Multiple recent reports cite declining morale, insubordination, indiscipline, and even mutiny—all due to the humiliation that the Indian enlisted suffer at the hands of their officers. They clearly have a systemic trust and respect issue that will challenge their ability to master what the US succeeds at in many areas. I'm of the mind that you can learn something from anyone, even (especially) kids. And when you shut down that input and learning resource, you also shut down the trust and respect developed through that exchange.

> "I'm of the mind that you can learn something from anyone, even (especially) kids."

In that moment of stark clarity, I realized that it all came down to those two simple things—trust and respect. That is the secret ingredient that helps make the extraordinary and difficult even remotely possible. When I understood the culture that defined the Indian navy, I could also understand why they had such a hard time accepting how we teach people to do what we do on board US aircraft carriers. It also reinforced how powerful earned trust and respect is as a recognition tool.

Could trust, or the absence of it, have contributed to the end of the Cold War?

When Trust Dies

Having studied and prepared for a prolonged conventional war or, God forbid, a cataclysmic nuclear war with the Soviets, I knew that trust and respect were clearly missing in the Soviet military. Recalling history, I knew that the Russians became notorious for forming special

lines—right behind their front troop positions—with the singular purpose of shooting anyone who tried to retreat. No big deal: It was a
small price to pay to potentially change the course of the battle for Stalingrad against the Germans and preserve communism. Discounting the
1.1 million Russians who were killed, it worked so well at Stalingrad to
enhance "loyalty" and to defeat the enemy (including those who would
dare retreat) that the Russians thought, *Why not institutionalize such a
winning concept in a post–World War II Soviet Union?* Communism,
as it turns out, is more of an acquired taste, and it has to be force-fed.

That general feeling of mistrust permeated every facet of the post–
World War II Soviet communist recovery, but it was especially pronounced in the military for one very important reason—the Communist
Party feared, above all things, the threat posed by a professional military
force. In what ended up being their signature example of institutional-
ized mistrust, supervisory civilian personnel—known as political officers, or *Zampolits*—were embedded within nearly all military units and
had the authority to override a commander's decisions. Why? Because
they didn't want any rogue military commanders turning their weapons
against the "Party." To make matters a little more difficult for military
commanders, the *Zampolits* also placed a great deal of their emphasis
on junior personnel "indoctrination" and "education" as a counter to
potential independent thinking. The unintended consequence, of course,
was ineptness and mediocrity on a grand scale.

True tactical training and military readiness were displaced by political propaganda, irrational suspicion, and the constant fear of reprisal.
Promotions were predominantly based on the communist version of
"political correctness" rather than the more recognized standards for
military professionals of high morale, fighting fitness, tactical innovation, efficiency, trust, and respect. Not surprisingly, despite their intense
investment in an arms race against the West, the Russians' ability to

realistically use that investment as they intended became increasingly more limited as their vast network of mistrust compromised nearly everything. As military readiness and cohesiveness dissolved at the hands of the *Zampolits*, the military responded like any good communist party loyalist—they lied. There was no such thing as a bad report when it came to describing the health, welfare, and achievements of military units and their war fighting equipment. They became a true "hollow" force—a complete joke.

Mistrust was also rampant in Soviet weapon system design. Clearly, allowing a *Zampolit* to ride along was impractical in fighter and bomber aircraft. Still, I had often wondered, as I intercepted and then escorted Soviet bombers far out over the Pacific Ocean, if a *Zampolit* was ordering the flight crew to salute me with the middle finger, or hold up a handwritten sign asking for cigarettes, or try and get me to fly into the water at night or in poor weather. Having extensively studied the Soviet aircraft designs of that era, it seems pretty obvious that they were more worried about defections than performance. Imagine the political consequences for them should one occur—not only would their intense propaganda, indoctrination, and educational system be compromised, but also the "Party's" very survival would be in play.

When Autonomy Is Removed

So how would you design tactical aircraft for pilots you don't trust when you have no place in the plane to put a *Zampolit*? The answer is simple. Take away all autonomy and decision-making, make the cockpit a confusing mess, track them wherever they go, and make it impossible to do anything without ground control direction—the only place you could position a *Zampolit*. Now, as we all know, this approach didn't end well for the Soviets.

With the implosion of the Soviet Union and the end of the Cold War, it became very clear that we had grossly overestimated their true military capability. And it wasn't because their technology was inferior or that their pilots were incapable of complex air tactics. In my opinion, it was mainly because they were terminally undermined by trust issues.

There were signs of dysfunction well before the implosion, especially with their preferred international military arms customers, but we mostly chalked that up to incompetence. Operations against Iraq, Libya, and Syria highlighted their completely inept use of aircraft, tactics, and weapons. A typical Soviet fighter cockpit, from the pilot's perspective, was a mess. The things that most pilots value, such as radar and weapon system integration, were placed in odd and awkward places and provided little or no situational awareness. Their jets were analogous to the Griswold family's car in the movie *National Lampoon's Vacation*.

"The two contrasting trust approaches produced significantly different results in combat. The difference is not even close."

So why would anyone purposely design a death trap? Well, it only makes sense when you inventory the Soviets' biggest fear: the threat posed by a professional military force. If defection prevention is the primary objective, and if the military can control aircraft from the ground, complete with a *Zampolit*, there is no need for all those fancy cockpit extravagances—and that is exactly what the Soviets did. This also explains their fascination with and dependence on "data link," the system that modern air forces use to share information with one another, manage air battles, and even fly aircraft remotely.

The Soviets seemed to be very advanced and disciplined with its use. We originally considered it a sign of sophistication and technical superiority, but we were wrong. It was simply a distrust feature that allowed them to drive every action from the ground. The Soviets were basically using pilots for the more tedious tasks of takeoff and landing, and then as a backup to their ground control. In contrast, Western aircraft are designed to provide an air crew with the highest quality tactical information, in the most easily assimilated display format, so they can manage the air war right from their cockpit. The two contrasting trust approaches produced significantly different results in combat. The difference is not even close.

I could go on about how the absence of trust and respect at the personal level, the team level, and the national level will create adverse and insidious consequences that limit creativity, competence, performance, and aspiration, but I think the implosion of the Soviet Union and the end of the Cold War is a fairly powerful testament as to the low probability of extraordinary achievement without them.

Awards, medals, trophies, citations, and other forms of recognition are great, but to truly serve the very best interests of children, they must also be linked with an appropriate dose of earned trust and respect. And when they don't, it is also important to distinguish the difference.

When You Fail to Contain the Risk

When I was faced with a very tragic incident as an F/A-18 squadron commanding officer, it was understanding the importance of trust that helped me frame my immediate response and move the squadron forward.

I was blessed with a very talented, professional, and inspired team that I completely trusted and respected, especially my maintenance department. One night off the coast near San Diego, as I was sitting in the ready room during the first night launch, one of my maintenance officers approached me, leaned over, and whispered in my ear, "Skipper, I think we just lost a jet." Almost simultaneously, I felt the ship turn hard, and the announcements that followed confirmed the worst. One of my jets was in the water. All I knew at the time was that it was extremely dark, it was my newest pilot, and it happened on launch. The longest night in my life had just begun.

As more information trickled in, it didn't appear that the pilot had attempted an ejection. Nonetheless, I joined the captain on the bridge, and we mounted an aggressive search-and-rescue mission. As the night progressed, hope for a happy ending slowly faded, and we still had no idea what potentially caused the crash. Was something wrong with the aircraft? Was something wrong with the catapult? Was it the pilot? Would we ever know? In the middle of the night, I assembled the entire squadron. Their faces and body language were not what I was accustomed to seeing. The pride, confidence, and fighting spirit they normally projected as a natural expression of their hard-earned trust and respect had been clearly vanquished. In that critical moment, I felt that my most important task was to get that back.

> " . . . the only thing I could think to do was to remind them why they had earned my trust and respect in the first place—and why they still enjoyed it."

As we gathered as a family, grieving the probable loss of a shipmate and dealing with the agonizing guilt that the team was feeling because they assumed they had failed somehow, the only thing I could think to do was to remind them why they had earned my trust and respect in the first place—and why they still enjoyed it. I ended with my personal assurance that there wasn't one of their jets that I wouldn't get in and fly immediately because of my confidence in their professionalism and their superior maintenance legacy. I also reminded them we still had a mission to perform, independent of the crash.

As darkness gave way to light, we had only recovered the digital flight recorder and the pilot's helmet. The pilot and aircraft were gone. In the last bit of darkness, I made the hardest phone call I have ever made—telling a young man's mother that she would never see him again. A sunrise memorial service was quickly organized in the hangar, and an aircraft was readied for me to fly back to our home base to handle all the details that come with such a tragedy.

Staying true to my word from the night before, I approached the jet I was scheduled to use. In violation of policy, I did something I had never done prior or ever have since—I just got in and started it up without inspecting the jet. Knowing that this was the first launch following the crash and that all eyes were on me, I took the opportunity to communicate through action that I trusted and respected everyone responsible for maintaining that jet—and everyone else should too. I showed them how respect and trust can be used to repair and heal.

The investigation that followed determined that all of the aircraft systems were fully functional but ultimately revealed that the pilot had suffered from an overpowering visual illusion that forced him to push the nose of the airplane down—despite what his instruments and warning alarms were telling him. Being so low to the water left him no chance for a recovery. Just as a parent would, I often think through the options available to me that would have prevented this tragic accident. I've come to the conclusion that despite our best efforts to manage and control all risk, it can never truly be completely contained.

Why You Have to Celebrate Too

We have examined the diverse and complex nature of recognition and reward. It is also worthwhile and essential to blend in some celebration. What do you celebrate? When do you celebrate? How big do you celebrate?

I put celebrations in the same category as thankfulness and contrition. It is better to do too much rather than too little. If in doubt, celebrate, give thanks, and say you're sorry. I may be wrong, but with my celebration approach, not only do I get to recognize, inventory, and honor all the past challenges, obstacles, and setbacks my team and I have had to overcome, but I also get to honor those I've depended on—and even those I may have offended along the way.

Real celebrations create an emotional reference point that can help project you into the future. Like mile markers in a marathon, clearing each one reinforces your commitment to your journey and helps discipline your mind to override what your body is telling it to do—*stop*. At the memorial service, we celebrated our fallen pilot's life and journey and used his premature death to harvest the important lessons that would improve our own journey going forward. With each real celebration, no matter how slight, you continuously reinforce the importance of discipline in pursuit of your goals.

We are always looking for something to celebrate in our house—passing a hard math test, backing the car out of the garage without hitting anything, high scores on video games, promotions—and sometimes we just celebrate for the hell of it. Just getting through a tough day, for example. But the biggest and most unbelievable celebration I've ever experienced is returning home from deployment. There is no equivalent to the emotional surge of reuniting with one's family and friends after months of separation, while simultaneously being relieved of the stress of combat operations and high-risk flight environments. It gets even better if it coincides with seeing a new son or daughter for the first time. Celebrations of this magnitude overwhelm the senses and live on with no regard to time.

Guides to Celebrations

As great as celebrations can be, and as numerous as they should be, there are some very important guidelines I recommend following.

☆ The first and most important is that you should never celebrate the suffering, humiliation, or misfortune of others, no matter how much you think they deserve it. Although it might seem satisfying to delight in the failures of the bullies of the world, or the over-reach of the affluent, or even the miscalculations of your competitors, in those situations, celebration is dangerously misplaced—it shifts the focus on their mistakes and karma reckoning rather than your accomplishments. There is no reward or nobility in celebrating anything other than the perseverance and discipline that has allowed someone to achieve the extraordinary.

☆ There is a half-life for celebrations. The quicker you can celebrate the achievement, the more powerful the emotional impact. The more powerful the emotional impact, the more powerful and calibrated are the discipline, commitment, and aspiration elements that drive the aggressiveness and reach of the next achievement.

☆ Timeliness is always more important than extravagance and level of participation. Don't sacrifice the real benefits of celebration for any lesser ones if doing so will incur unreasonable delays. And in all cases, it is still better to celebrate late than never.

☆ My final celebratory guideline is scalability. All achievements and levels of effort are not equal, and therefore the scope and size of the celebration must match. A high five or fist bump may be just fine for some achievements, while other feats might demand a little more investment, preparation time, and pomp and circumstance. And just like recognition inflation, celebration inflation can be counter-productive. If you can picture the over-the-top promotion celebrations that Adam Sandler experienced in the movie *Billy Madison*, you can quickly grasp the concept through the extreme. In my opinion, it is better to go light when unsure. In time, most kids end up having a fairly good perspective on recognition, reward, and celebration, and they end up focusing their mind, heart, and spirit on what truly produces personal and team achievement rather than the random and unpredictable spoils that may follow. Happiness, my final subject, is highly dependent on parent mastery of family recognition, reward, and celebration.

☆☆☆

FIGHTER PILOT PARENT TAKEAWAYS— Recognition, Rewards, and Celebrations

☆ Recognition can be a powerful performance enhancer. With every birthday celebration, we try to bring attention to annual achievement and adversity management rather than just a trip around the sun.

☆ Subjective recognition criteria are inherently unfair. Since beauty is in the eye of the beholder, kids should never expect recognition and be prepared to humbly return it when it is not deserved. And in all cases, recognition should be shared with the team.

★ Keep recognition inflation in check. As a fighter pilot parent, one method I use is to have my kids tell me three things they did well and three things they could have done better. Think about it—you can always find three things, no matter what the context. It helps to keep recognition in perspective, and it helps them become their own best and honest critic.

★ Objective recognition criteria require constant updates. "That was great! Now let's see if you can do a little bit more . . . " and so on.

★ If someone is recognized for something you did, don't sweat it; the right people already know. As a coach I always tried to recognize the kid that set up the play that led to a score rather than the kid who scored the goal. The goal scorer always gets recognized.

★ If you receive undue recognition, set the record straight and give credit to those who deserve it. It helps to reflect on those moments when you failed to be recognized for a significant contribution or achievement and how it made you feel. The emotional impact should be the same or worse when you get credit for something you didn't do.

★ Without some autonomy or spontaneity for a unique or timely significant contribution or achievement, the trust and respect quotient is muted.

★ The highest form of recognition is earned trust and respect. From a kid's perspective, this occurs when they get more play time, extra privileges, or are asked to lead others through a routine or problem. Remind them that they are receiving the highest form of recognition.

★ Trust and respect are also useful to repair and heal confidence setbacks. A fighter pilot parent will get kids right back out there, not only to redeem themselves, but to also demonstrate trust and respect for them.

★ Celebrate any achievement that demanded discipline, perseverance, and mastery of something new. We've celebrated juggling, high video game scores, and even arduous hikes. As long as the celebration theme is journey-focused, it's worth celebrating.

★ Never celebrate the misfortunes of others. I remind my kids that there is no glory or benefit to be found in the misery and suffering of others.

★ The more quickly you celebrate an achievement, the better. Victory laps take place immediately after the race for a reason.

★ Scale the celebration to the achievement to keep celebration inflation in check. Not everything warrants a new car.

CHAPTER NINE

GUIDING CHILDREN TOWARD HAPPINESS

Happiness does not have to be elusive. I've experienced firsthand some of the happiest and most generous people in the world who literally had nothing in terms of material possessions. I've also experienced firsthand some of the most miserable and troubled people in the world who were blessed with abundant material wealth and opportunity. How can this be? What do the happy and content know that others don't? Is wealth a curse? And probably the most important question: What can you do as a parent to help your children become legitimately and perpetually happy and content?

As Americans, we often view the world through a prism that reflects our own personal experiences, culture, and elevated sense of what a normal life is. We enjoy freedom, liberty, a relatively high standard of living, and abundance. Per the World Bank's data and analysis on global inequality, we are decisively blessed. In America, as discomforting as this fact may be to the bottom 5 percent of people, they are still decisively richer than *68 percent* of the rest of the world and would be considered rich by India's standards. The poorest continent, Africa, is home to twenty-one of the world's top twenty-five poorest countries[7]. It should be no surprise that people want to come to the United States. It is clearly the land of opportunity.

Yet the United States ranks only eighteenth on the World Happiness Map.[8] According to the World Health Organization, the United States is in the top three of the most mentally depressed countries, just behind China and India. That's right, countries like Bangladesh, Nigeria, Mexico, and Russia have lower rates of depression, anxiety, alcoholism, and drug abuse.[9] What gives? Why are Americans not happier?

Having been to many of the world's poorest places, I was absolutely astonished to experience happy and smiling people wherever I went, independent of wealth or status. How could they be happy without experiencing McDonald's or Disneyland?

Priceless Lessons from Africa

On my first visit to Africa, a group from my squadron decided to go on safari. Not the hunting kind, but the touring kind. On the second day of our port visit to Mombasa, in the very early morning hours, eight of us rushed to board one of only sixty or so dedicated minivans that had assembled along a busy city street in support of our special USS *Enterprise* tour package. We were extremely satisfied that not only had we secured a van, but we were still all together! We relaxed and waited for the main body of the caravan to finish loading so we could commence the three-day African adventure just before sunrise.

---

7   Tim Worstall, "Astonishing Numbers: America's Poor Still Live Better Than Most Of The Rest Of Humanity," June 1, 2013. *Forbes*, https://www.forbes.com/sites/timworstall/2013/06/01/astonishing-numbers-americas-poor-still-live-better-than-most-of-the-rest-of-humanity/#6437e2cf54ef

8   WorldLifeExpectancy, https://www.worldlifeexpectancy.com/world-happiness-map

9   Deirdre McPhillips, "U.S. Among Most Depressed Countries in the World," *US News and World Report*, September 14, 2016. https://www.usnews.com/news/best-countries/articles/2016-09-14/the-10-most-depressed-countries

In the relatively low light of western Mombasa, the trail of tour-bound headlights was impressive as it snaked through the hills of a dark and quiet landscape. Although the van we were in was neither quiet, comfortable, nor clean, it was ours, and it was taking us on a once-in-a-lifetime experience. We could deal with anything!

Getting Lost

At one point, those of us who were still awake soon noticed that our van had started slowing down and the other vans were passing us. From there, things got rapidly worse, and then the noise started. We felt and heard a loud metallic clunking beneath our feet. Clearly something was seriously wrong. But the driver seemed oblivious to it as he smiled and pressed on. And then, just as the sun started to leak light to the east, the bottom fell out—literally. Something of considerable size separated from our vehicle, and we came to an immediate stop.

We piled out of the van along the narrow shoulder of a two-lane road and looked at each other in disbelief. As the driver took out his flashlight, the remnants of what used to be our van's drivetrain reflected back to us in several pieces. Between the multiple engineers among us, we collectively concluded that there was no way that our van would ever be driveable again. Meanwhile, as we stood contemplating our situation, our driver became engaged in a high-pitched and rapid discussion on his radio, presumably to work out a recovery plan.

As the sun broke over the horizon, we surveyed the damage. The U-joint had clearly failed, and the driveshaft had separated from the car. As the driver finished his last transmission on the radio, he smiled at us and gave us a thumbs-up. Could our trip be salvaged? As we waited to find out, we became acutely aware of movement around us.

Remembering that we were in Africa, our immediate and mostly irrational concern became large predators, so we retreated toward the van. While establishing our defensive position around the vehicle, we scanned our surroundings through the dim morning light. We spotted a bunch of grass huts elevated on stilts. As the sunrise continued to reveal more details, the movement that we initially feared as large African predators was actually small people—children. Highly curious, they cautiously surveilled us from a safe distance.

We found ourselves in a small village that had awakened to a rare oddity. With the threat of being eaten extinguished and the hope of a quick van fix tempered, our curiosity quickly matched that of the children who were watching us, so we invited them to join our circle. The crowd quickly grew as we became the center of village attention. Absent a common language, we used hand gestures, drew pictures in the dirt, and pointed to things in order to communicate. Curiosity soon gave way to fascination, which then gave way to human connection. In communal fashion, we shared snacks from the ship plus a version of the popular game of Pente.

"Even more shocking was that they also appeared to be very happy and content. How could that be? They had nothing, right?"

Pente is a simple board game that uses a grid and beads in a system that allows you to achieve a win if you can place five beads in sequence—diagonally, horizontally, or vertically. We had everything we needed to re-create it where we were: dirt and a stick to make the grid and enough rocks for everyone in Africa to play. After demonstrating the rules, the kids quickly picked it up and then mastered the strategy and tactics after only a couple of rounds. Multiple matches propagated around Pente ground zero, and despite the language barrier, we were easily communicating with one another.

As we got a chance to observe our fellow gamers, we could easily see that their existence was clearly challenging. They lived in huts, they had no running water or sanitation system, they didn't appear to have a school, and most didn't have shoes. Yet they appeared to be healthy with bright eyes and bright smiles, and they were obviously very intelligent. Even more shocking was that they also appeared to be very happy and content. How could that be? They had nothing, right?

Fully immersed in fellowship with our new friends, we barely noticed the hours slipping by or our rescue team's arrival. Expecting a replacement van, we became suspicious when the rescue driver handed a small box to our driver, along with some tools, then drove off. In the box was a U-joint saturated in grease and several bolts. The driver immediately started assembling parts and after dropping the U-joint in the dirt a few times (thus covering it with a collection of small rocks and sand), he started to resuscitate our dead vehicle as we looked on in disbelief.

We mentally questioned the selected solution and pondered our fate should the vehicle fail again in the bush. But we finally conceded and offered a helping hand to make sure the repair was performed properly (not that any of us were trained mechanics). Aside from the hard work to remove debris from the grease and an extra part or two, we were able to get everything back together and—to our amazement and pride—everything actually worked. If not for this and a few more experiences that followed, my perspective on happiness may have been perpetually flawed.

It seemed odd that after only spending a few hours in this unknown village with complete strangers who we couldn't talk to, we were reluctant to move on. Despite their economic plight, their genuine and profound joy and happiness was contagious and heartwarming and knew no language barrier. After hugging the children and shaking hands with the elders, we loaded up again and sadly pressed on in our freshly rejuvenated safari-mobile.

Alone on the road again and moving into uncharted hostile territory, we would soon learn that our breakdown and delay was a huge blessing in disguise (beyond that of our engagement with the Village of the Happy). Hours behind the main body of our group (which we hoped to rejoin at the first watering hole where lunch awaited), we spotted a large convoy of white vans coming toward us in the distance. As we approached in the opposite direction on the very narrow dirt road, we became acutely aware of one of the key hazards associated with convoy safari tours—the immense dust cloud that sixty vans could create.

It wouldn't be too bad for a first van, but the fifty-nine that followed were consumed by it. Had we been in the middle of the pack, as before, we wouldn't have been able to see anything, and we may have even choked to death on the thick African dirt. The thrill that we had anticipated of reuniting with our group was quickly converted to revulsion as we barely survived the dust of the convoy passing by. We quickly decided that we would rather be eaten by a lion alongside our broken-down safari-mobile than to breathe that much dirt for the next three days. So now, solo for the rest of the trip, we had freedoms we wouldn't have had otherwise.

The van, our only hope of survival, held up surprisingly well—until it started overheating. To manage this new situation, we were forced to take tactical pauses to replenish coolant and drove at forty miles per hour. At each pause, we were truly in the bush, and predators were visible all around us. Our driver freaked out if we moved any more than a foot or two away from the vehicle. We figured he had had an unfortunate incident with a passenger that he clearly didn't want to relive. Our spastic migration across the expansive Kenyan savannah prevented even the slightest chance of joining up with our main body.

Getting Found

On day two, as we entered the massive Shetani Lava Flow, we came across a lone hitchhiker, dressed in a pin-striped suit, sandals, and carrying a small sack. The suit was atypical—it had short sleeves, and the pinstripes were horizontal instead of vertical. Although the driver protested, we stopped and picked him up. Sitting between the driver and me, I couldn't take my eyes off our guest's ears. The bottom part of both his earlobes were detached from the main ear, and if not lassoed around the top part of the ear, they would dangle four to five inches below the ear. The driver explained, in broken English, that our guest rider was a Maasai warrior returning from vacation. Fascinated by who he was and the fact that the Maasai took vacations, we tried to bridge the language divide and find out more.

The first thing we discovered was that he didn't like candy. After placing our gift of a piece of butterscotch hard candy in his mouth, he immediately spit it out and started digging frantically in his sack. He pulled out a twig that had been methodically chewed on one end until it bristled. Not sure what he was doing or why, we watched in amazement as he placed the bristled end of the twig in his mouth. Then, using what we determined to be a bush-fashioned toothbrush, he vigorously attempted to remove all history of that offensive butterscotch candy from his body. Fortunately, he liked the biscuits we offered much better.

During our long ride together, we were able to develop an understanding of his life, his people, and his culture. The Maasai are very proud and very traditional, and they are the most authentic ethnic tribe in Kenya and Tanzania. The boys are on a steady path to "warrior" status, and their primary purpose is to protect their cattle from humans and predators. The women are taught to build houses and do beadwork. As nomadic cattle custodians, their houses are usually small, semipermanent circular dwellings built from mud, grass, wood, and the key ingredient, cow dung. Some of their villages have a wall of sharpened, outward-projecting sticks to protect them from predators. And as we slowly learned more about their unique culture and way of life, our desire to spend time with them intensified.

Exiting the lava flows, we started to encounter more and more humans. We eventually arrived at our hitchhiker's village, which looked like perfect grazing land for their cattle. He clearly had A-list standing, and we were crowd-rushed by his many admirers. The crowd quieted and listened intently as we presumably were introduced. Our transition from suspicious outsiders to revered guests happened almost instantaneously, followed by our own special crowd rush. The Maasai's normal dress is bright and festive, which elevated our once-in-a-lifetime experience even further. We took advantage of our special status and accepted their hand-signaled invitation to get an insider's perspective of their day-to-day lives. By American standards, they lived a poor, humble, and challenging existence, with the added benefit of a 24/7 manure smell. They should have been sad, dejected, depressed, and miserable. But they weren't. In fact, they were the complete opposite. They were proud, noble, dignified, joyous, and happy.

Getting Real

As with our earlier villager experience, their happiness defied logic and was simultaneously contagious. It was also a source of great shame and embarrassment to me. I must confess that none of my many personal meltdowns or mood swings over the years had been caused by anything even closely resembling the discomfort, suffering, or scarcity that these good people endured every day. And yet they were still happy and vibrant and loved life. I needed some of that.

Although I realized that true happiness had nothing to do with power, money, comfort, or toys, I couldn't quite put my finger on what these extraordinary people did to choose happy every day. It became much clearer after I met Joe Caruso, the author of *The Power of Losing Control*—an interesting story about his battle with cancer and how that experience changed his life. Through that trial of will, pain, suffering, hopelessness, fatigue, and near death, he emerged on the other side as a full-fledged Maasai warrior, so to speak. He had figured out how to choose happiness despite it all. Easier said than done, you think?

Through my experiences as a fighter pilot and my close examinations of happy people who have no reason to be happy, I've developed an understanding and approach that I personally deploy and share with my children. My approach requires first accepting the reality that happiness is a state of mind, and you, therefore, determine if you are happy or not. Not anyone else.

Becoming an Active Participant in Our Own Happiness

I think that most people's resistance to making the choice to be happy has to do with either the illusion of control or the perceived lack of control. Eventually, the people who think they have control—and therefore have high expectations of favorable outcomes—are frequently angry, upset, and inconsolable when their plans don't work out. Despite being perpetually reminded of how little control they actually command, the emotional biases they have been nurturing over many years can often prevent proper recalibration. Conversely, the people who don't think they have any control at all often fail to recognize and use the power they do have. Everyone has power . . . up to a point.

You have the power to control the magnitude and direction of your energy, focus, intellect, and faith. You can construct more power. You can increase or intensify the magnitude and direction of your power through discipline, education, and health. But that is where your power and control starts and stops.

Being a fighter pilot makes this painfully obvious. The lack of total control seems to be punctuated during every flight hour, every mission, every emergency, and every takeoff and landing. Although it would be nice, we can't control weather, the enemy, the laws of physics, the thousands of parts that propel us through the air, or the number and frequency of full moons at night. And hoping for sympathy, compliance, or a free pass from those things we can't control, at least in that environment, is a proven path to disaster. You quickly learn that either the illusion of control or the failure to assert control tends to be unforgiving. At least fighter pilots have one additional control that most people do not have: an ejection seat. And no, I've never had to use one. But that doesn't mean pilots shouldn't when conditions demand they do.

"At least fighter pilots have one additional control that most people do not have: an ejection seat."

Have you ever met an unhappy fighter pilot? My guess is probably not. And part of the reason is that fighter pilots realize quite early in their development that their very survival and success depends on maximizing the magnitude and direction of what they can control while fully honoring the things they can't. With that framework to guide them, their sphere of control continues to grow as their respect for the things they can't grows too.

So the first secret of choosing happiness starts with a focus on and investment in the things you can control and leveraging those controls as your source of power to change your destiny. Will you still fail? Most definitely, but your response will drive you forward, not backward. I'm sure you know people who have this quality. They're the ones who get back up when they get knocked down.

Each time they get back up, their source of control and power expands, along with their ability to choose happiness. Every one of my kids has failed at something and wanted to quit immediately, but the fighter pilot parent in me knows that quitting can become a habit just as easily as getting back at it can become a habit. For all the things kids do, helping them get back up when they fall helps them develop the proper happiness habits.

> "Each time they get back up, their source of control and power expands, along with their ability to choose happiness."

For kids, whether it's sports, academics, music, or relationships, this becomes an important understanding. Instead of being a spectator who depends on either luck or the good grace of others to drive their desired outcomes, they become an active and disciplined participant in their own life.

Making this critical shift in processing the external world drives children to work more exclusively on the things they can control, which ultimately leads to better results and the complete ownership of their future and fortunes. It also makes them better leaders. There is a wide variation in describing what a leader is and how to develop into one, but for me, it really comes down to a basic understanding of control limitations. To be a great leader (or parent), you must be able to inspire and compel others to contribute their independent energy, focus, intellect, and faith—with sufficient magnitude and direction—in pursuit of extraordinary goals and extraordinary achievements.

Making the Extraordinary Look Easy

When we fail to acknowledge the limits of our own control, we will typically fail to appreciate and respect the value and potential contribution represented by others, which automatically limits our own prospects. Fighter pilots, SEALs, and any other high-performing groups who are commonly recognized for making the extraordinary look easy are actually very ordinary people who work extremely hard to develop and expand their own tools, while inspiring others to join with them with different tools, in order to build a complete toolbox that can handle big and challenging jobs.

Happiness flows from this community of inspired contributions and the intersection of a common and noble vision for the future. By honoring and respecting the critical people you need on your team, inspiring them instead of commanding them or merely hoping for their contribution, you dramatically change the realm of the possible and the high probability of choosing happiness—independent of barriers, adversity, or sacrifice. Martin Luther King Jr. was brilliant at this. His ability to win over the hearts, minds, and fighting spirit of millions of very diverse people in support of civil rights set the high-water mark for leadership.

The Past: Where the Enemies of Happiness Live

Understanding the nature of your true power has one other happiness benefit: You start to focus on the now and the future rather than the past. That's important, because the past is where you will find many enemies of happiness—resentment, revenge, anger, inadequacy, insecurity, doubt, and the emotional basis and bias for avoiding the things you need to do in the now. Harvest the lessons of the past, but lock the rest of it into a maximum-security prison. You act and make a difference in the now, so don't obsess about things you have no power to control. Your energy, focus, intellect, and faith will potentially shape the future but won't necessarily define it. Anxiousness, nervousness, and anticipation are all symptoms of our minds reconciling adverse outcomes before they ever happen.

These emotions can be very powerful and a distraction to what you can do in the now—and therefore a distraction to happiness. Kids are especially vulnerable during transition from middle school to high school, moving to a new area, or when negotiating new social situations. When we moved our son to a new middle school, he was very upset on his first day. He had already decided that no one would like him. And since he didn't know anybody on the first day, the adverse outcome he anticipated became his reality. So I made a deal with him. He had to introduce himself to five kids and then tell me a quick but detailed narrative about each of them. If after that, he still wanted to go back to his old school, I'd honor his wish. By Friday, not only did he want to stay at his new school, but he was also able to talk about ten or so of his new friends.

For fighter pilots who land on aircraft carriers, there are an infinite number of bad things that could happen in the immediate future. Imagining all the possible ways of dying or failing to perform is simply demoralizing, paralyzing, and counterproductive. I freely admit that I drifted in that direction several times: approaching each check ride, my first carrier landing, my first night carrier landing, my first time in combat, my first day as a squadron commander—and my first day as a parent. It never ends.

Moving Back to Now

Managing fear, as we discussed earlier, is really a process of moving back to the now, where you have power and control. And the now includes risk management features (backup plans) should the future get unacceptably ugly. My son's power and control at his new school was established by talking to kids he didn't know and by asking questions and listening to their answers in order to learn enough to satisfy my challenge. His backup plan was to engage different kids until he got to at least five, and his backup to his backup—his equivalent of an ejection seat handle—was his old school. Fortunately, it didn't come to that.

Insurance Policies and Ejection Seats

How do you leverage your power and control in the now to help you choose happy? You "buy" insurance and peace of mind in the now. My son's insurance included one hundred or more classmates to choose from. Having evolved in a profession with a seemingly endless sequence of "must not fail" missions, getting the now right makes all the difference in the world. The now is where you insure against failure with both redundancy and contingency plans for the most probable and severe threats to your future success. It is similar to a home equity line of credit. If you need it, you have access to it. If not, even better. When you master your now, the benefits are immediate—doing so gives you comfort, peace of mind, and the ability to choose happy. How did I know my son would choose happy? How did I know the quest for five new friends would bear fruit? Well, I knew my son, and I knew how people responded to those who listen to them when they talk about themselves. I considered the "ejection" option a very remote possibility.

Generally speaking, that still may not be enough for some people—particularly those who are blessed with affluence, wealth, and an enviable quality of life. It seems ironic that the more you have, the harder you have to work at happiness. This paradox is actually very human and requires discipline to overcome. Think about it. It is very tough mentally to downgrade to a Ford Focus after having owned a Corvette. Every time you upgrade, so does your expectation of minimum acceptability. Unfortunately, for some this escalation is very closely linked to happiness. What if you lost everything, or you had to recalibrate your standard of minimum acceptability—could you still choose happy?

Recalibrating with kids can be even worse. I've struggled to teach my kids how to decouple happiness from material things since so many of their friends have no realistic sense of what a "want" is compared to a "need." Our kids don't get the latest iPhone or clothing styles the moment they come out, but they do get opportunities to explore their passions through sports and hobbies—and also serve others through charitable organizations that they care about. This helps place "want" and "need" into proper perspective. Many of their friends ask for and receive anything they *want* with no consideration to the corrosive effects waged on true happiness. This goes way beyond being spoiled when happiness is totally correlated to the immediate gratification of a want fulfillment. It is tough for parents to be disciplined about balancing the want versus need equation, especially if they have lost the battle themselves. But if they aren't, over time, they lose their ability to genuinely be thankful and appreciative for what they receive and what they already have, which makes happiness an elusive and moving target.

> "It is tough for parents to be disciplined about balancing the want versus need equation, especially if they have lost the battle themselves."

If you lost 10 percent of everything you own, could you find something to be thankful for and appreciative of? How about 50 percent? Ninety percent? What about 100 percent? Tough task, right? Yet people have setbacks all the time, and they have no choice but to find a way to deal with it. And dealing with it always starts with finding something to be thankful for and appreciative of, which may even include . . . *gulp* . . . the series of events and mistakes that created the situation they now find themselves in.

"Choosing happiness starts with lowering your standards and replacing your happiness igniters with things that you can never lose or are unlikely to lose."

When my kids started writing essays for college applications, they often cited moving across the country as a setback or challenge that ultimately became a blessing that they were thankful for. It allowed them to see and experience different parts of the country and helped them to develop good social strategies, leadership skills, and confidence. Choosing happiness is tough enough on a good day, but how do you make that choice when something that represents happiness to you is no longer available? Choosing happiness starts with lowering your standards and replacing your happiness igniters with things that you can never lose or are unlikely to lose.

Take Inventory of What You Take for Granted

The first step is to inventory everything you take for granted. Make a list. This could include anything from friends and family and food and shelter to those unique skills and talents you developed and mastered long ago. Second, inventory the mistakes, failures, setbacks, and disappointments that led you to greater wisdom—the things that forced you to change an existing path to one that ultimately led to better opportunities and outcomes and was more closely aligned to your passion. Lastly, observe what's around you in the external world and recognize every detail of beauty that pleases the senses. Your list might include leaves changing colors in the fall, sunsets, waves pounding the shoreline—even city skylines and majestic buildings. The one thing all these things have in common is that they will be there for you when other things come and go. When you ritualize this inventory process and recognize the value that each one contributes to your life, no matter how slight, a genuine sense of gratitude, thankfulness, and appreciation will follow. Once you achieve this state, you can simultaneously acknowledge grace and choose happiness.

Ritualizing a Family Inventory List

With my kids, we do this in a number of ways. Our inventory list receives top thankfulness billing in our prayers and in our daily expressions of observation as we compare and contrast what the less fortunate are experiencing. My kids have now experienced firsthand the devastation of California wildfires and the tragic and senseless loss of life in the November 2018 shooting at the Borderline Bar and Grill in Thousand Oaks, California. While our family was not directly threatened in those situations, their friends and our community definitely were. My children's inventory list now includes our family being spared. We make it a point to hug each other and say "I love you" whenever one of us leaves or comes home. We support each other and remind ourselves that setbacks are never permanent. And we try to find humor anywhere we can. In this kind of environment, material things lose value, setbacks create new opportunities, and we try not to take ourselves too seriously.

continued

Choosing happiness is never automatic, but it certainly becomes much easier when you ritualize behaviors that reinforce your search for it.

How to Predestine Happiness

As an air wing landing signal officer, I was responsible for the landing performance and safety of all pilots in my air wing. My duties included, among other things, controlling every landing on board the USS *Abraham Lincoln*, and then debriefing each pilot immediately afterward in their ready room. One day I would fly, and the next day I would spend my time alternating between the back of the ship during landings and walking through each ready room debriefing pilots. The normal routine was to meet my team of pilot and LSOs fifteen minutes prior to each recovery, and then check all the recovery-related equipment while the flight deck was being set up for landing. Once I had a "ready" deck, we would control each aircraft safely to landing, followed by a quick team debrief after the last aircraft in the recovery group was safely on board. Then the fun started. Since each landing was graded, we would visit each ready room, debrief the pilots, and then tell them their grade. After doing this every other day for eight months, it became very easy to predict individual and squadron happiness levels. Some squadrons were clearly much better at choosing happy than others, despite being subjected to very similar challenges and adversity.

The happier squadrons had a completely different ready room atmosphere. They usually had more people congregating there just for fellowship, and they were quick with a smile and a joke. Even more interesting, their landing grades were generally better, and they tended to be less disagreeable when they received a lower than expected grade. It really came down to leadership and how teams were taught to manage their happiness value system. The example was set by the more senior pilots and emulated by the newer pilots. They were quick to rebound and choose happy even if they didn't agree with their grade.

Less happier squadrons were miserable places to visit. They were like ghost towns where nobody hung out unless people absolutely had to be there. The pilots contested every grade they got, either verbally or with intensely defensive body language. Smiles and humor were far and few between. Some squadrons were so bad that I only let my most experienced LSOs debrief their pilots. Quite honestly, it all came down to a leadership failure. Senior pilots not only had a poor sense of personal control limits, but they also grossly overweighed their landing grades in their happiness calculations. Independent of what landing grade they had earned, they only seemed to choose happy if they received the highest grade possible. Set up for frequent disappointment, happiness was a tough choice for squadrons like this. To make matters worse, their adversarial attitude made it much less likely that they would ever get the benefit of the doubt in the future. Unknowingly, their limited ability to manage the discipline and perspective needed to choose happy was compromising their success trajectory. Plus, they weren't having much fun. I'm pretty sure they would not have made good Maasai warriors.

Helping Kids Project Power

I find myself repeatedly helping my kids identify where they have power and what they can control. If they are doing everything they can in the moments they have available to them, then that is all they can do. From academics and soccer time at college to plotting the course for their desired future, my greatest value seems to be helping them to project

their power in the most effective way. I usually start with a few important but simple questions:

* What do you seek?
* What do you need to get there?
* What can you do now to advance?

For parents, this is an important and essential prescription for leading children through the happiness process. Your kids need you to guide
them and set the example so that they are predestined to choose happiness throughout their lives.

Service to Others

The final leg of the happiness triangle is probably the easiest—being of
service to others. Think about the last time you helped someone and
how it made you feel. It probably didn't matter if you needed just as
much help as the people you assisted. The feeling of joy, accomplishment, and satisfaction is unmatched when you help somebody. It is so
strong that you almost feel embarrassed for feeling that good. Writing
a check to charity doesn't quite do it. You need to get in there and get
your hands dirty to fully experience the happiness benefit. The beauty
of it is that there are no minimum service levels required to activate that
feeling. Whether it is holding open a door for someone, carrying bags
for a senior citizen, or donating a kidney, you will get a boost in your
happiness level regardless.

This theme was pounded into my head relentlessly as a young
fighter pilot. "Troops first" and "Take care of your wingman" were our

nonnegotiable standards. In combat, we gave our highest support priority to ground forces that had become exposed and vulnerable. Even if we were out of ordnance, we would use the only thing we had left—speed and noise—to distract the enemy.

Service to others was paramount for career success and also peace of mind. Since a Navy fighter squadron was in continuous motion, moving to and from the ship and to and from other training sites, we would never rest or relax until everyone had a place to sleep, a place to eat, and felt comfortable with their new environment. Any officer who selfishly deviated from this service model stood out like a sore thumb and received unwanted and uncomfortable attention from their peers and seniors alike.

When Deployment Is Difficult

Returning home after long separations or from deployment was especially important in our service model. For most of us, the reunion with our families and the return to relative normalcy was reward enough for all our hard work. But for some, coming home meant something entirely different. Most often, that something meant having to reconcile a serious family or financial problem. While most of us were preparing for celebrations, a few valued members of our team were preparing for challenge and conflict. Our objective was to make sure that this particular group was fully supported during their transition before any of us could relax, rest, or celebrate.

Deployments are tough on all families, but for some they are devastating. Although purely anecdotal, I observed that the strain of separation and the subsequent manifestation of that stress led to a 5 percent divorce rate during a typical fighter squadron deployment. Many of these sailors were not aware of any problems at home until just a few days or weeks before their return date. The reality of the pending return at times forced very awkward communication—"It's over and don't come home." Since many of these very personal types of issues are rarely shared, even with close friends, we exerted great effort in preparing our leadership teams to be on the lookout for troubled shipmates and find ways to serve those that might be facing a very different type of homecoming.

Setting Up a Support Structure

We've all seen the news stories of families rushing and hugging their special pilot who just flew in, but you never see the sailor standing alone without family or friends as the celebratory crowds thin. In the service model I grew up in, we supported and served those sailors and became the family that should have been there for them.

This sense of service is not isolated to just those wearing the uniform. We also considered it unacceptable for any family member to suffer or struggle during deployment. We realized that it was nearly impossible for our sailors to focus on their mission if they were concerned about the people they cared most about back home. Grief and concern know no boundaries, and distance only magnifies the feeling of helplessness and frustration. In response, we embraced a service and support program dedicated to our families (mostly very young families) that were routinely left behind to fend for themselves.

In each squadron, there was a group of very special spouses—including the commanding and executive officers' spouses—who were trained to be ombudsmen. Their training prepared them to be experts in every form of health, employment, social, and financial aid program, and they were also responsible for family spirit and morale during deployments. They had direct access to the commanding officer who would engage with them at an executive level when the ombudsmen were unable to resolve an urgent issue. Their support ranged from helping to find child care for a new mom to coordinating a massive squadron picnic. Their service to others was tireless and often thankless and their contribution to combat readiness, although significant, was rarely factored in. But each one of them experienced the joy and happiness that came with each opportunity to serve someone else. To this day, my wife, a seasoned ombudsman, is extremely grateful for this opportunity because of the joy and satisfaction of helping others that she continues to benefit from when challenged to choose happy.

Supporting Your Wingman— on the Ground or in the Air

Things don't change in the air. It's difficult for me to think of a more time-honored or sacred responsibility for a fighter pilot than to serve and support your wingman. There is no quicker path to disgrace or humiliation than to fail in this role. The great majority of flight leaders from every generation not only dutifully and unconditionally served their own wingman as described, but they also extended this nonnegotiable commitment to any airborne colleague who finds themselves in extremis. One such gentleman is Medal of Honor recipient Tom Hudner. During the time he and I spent together at the commissioning of the USS *Stockdale*, he shared with me his personal firsthand account of the service he provided to his wingman, Jesse LeRoy Brown.

Tom was Jesse's wingman on December 4, 1950, flying the F4U-4 Corsair from the flight deck of the USS *Leyte*. Their mission that day was to suppress enemy fire in support of 8,000 desperate Marines fighting for survival at the "Frozen Chosin" Reservoir in North Korea. Tom was senior to Jesse, but Jesse led the fight because experience matters most in combat.

Tom and Jesse couldn't be from more different worlds. Tom was from New England; his parents made a comfortable and decent living; he graduated from the United States Naval Academy in 1946; and he was white.

Jesse, on the other hand, was the son of a poor Mississippi sharecropper and he was black. On his path to becoming a naval aviator, Jesse had to overcome a whole list of obstacles, including extreme hardship, inequality, and prejudice, just to survive—let alone become a Navy fighter pilot. His perseverance paid off.

Jesse was one of only a handful of black students at Ohio State University (now called The Ohio State University). He had to work nights loading boxcars to pay for school. Clearly, he was someone who understood both the limits and the power he controlled. From OSU, he painstakingly expanded the magnitude and direction of his energy, focus, intellect, and spirit to defy all odds by earning a Naval Reserve Officers Training Corps scholarship, and then he once again defied all odds when he became the very first black Navy pilot in 1948.

As impressive and awe-inspiring as those achievements were, they instantaneously became irrelevant when his engine failed following a direct antiaircraft artillery hit over enemy territory. With no engine and not enough altitude to bail out (he had no ejection seat), he was forced to make a "wheels up," "dead stick" landing in a small clearing on a snow-covered mountain slope. I suspect Jesse wasn't too worried about those things, since he had no power or control over them. It's a great example for parents when we are struggling to guide kids back toward constructive actions where they have the most power and control. All of

Jesse's efforts were dedicated to managing what he could control, which was limited to optimizing his rate of descent and aligning his approach to the best spot available, in order to keep both him and his aircraft from careening off the mountainside into certain death.

Tom, positioned above, helplessly watched Jesse's crash-landing and fully expected to see carnage during his subsequent flyby. As he rolled the aircraft to view and confirm the worst, he was shocked to see Jesse wave his arm from the mangled cockpit. The joy of seeing his wingman alive quickly turned to concern when he realized something was wrong. Jesse wasn't getting out and he wasn't moving, even though small fires were starting to build around him. "I'm going in," Tom radioed to his commander.

In that moment, Tom made the most unorthodox decision in the history of naval aviation. He decided to crash a perfectly good American fighter plane on a steep mountainside in an area controlled by an enthusiastic and committed enemy who had just shot down his wingman. Service to your wingman knows no price or sacrifice. As a fighter pilot parent, I feel exactly the same way toward my kids.

> "Service to your wingman knows no price or sacrifice. As a fighter pilot parent, I feel exactly the same way toward my kids."

So Tom, judging from Jesse's relative success in bringing in his aircraft, followed his lead. He oriented his flight path on a slightly offset trajectory that would bring him close to Jesse without plowing into him and then selected a landing point that was nearly identical. The fact that he was a Navy pilot who was used to landing on aircraft carriers most certainly boosted his confidence. This remote and rugged "landing strip" would be the largest landing area he had seen during the entire time of his deployment.

Tom masterfully controlled his airspeed, glideslope, and lineup as he fought the turbulent mountain air. Knowing he only had one chance to get it right, I'm sure he was comforted by the many times he had been in this situation during routine aircraft carrier operations. As he approached the point of no return, he braced for the jolting impact he fully expected— another routine landing experience for Navy pilots. With his wheels up, he cushioned the landing as best he could, then transitioned his plane into a sled. He was now at the complete mercy of terrain and snow.

Blinded and disoriented by snow wash, the violent ride that followed must have seemed like an eternity. As the plane eventually slowed and then abruptly came to a stop, Tom was surprised to see that his airplane's final parking spot was a mere 100 yards upslope of Jesse. Who would have guessed? If it had been a ship landing, Tom would have received the highest grade possible: "OK. No comment." Tom wasted no time getting to his friend and roommate.

As he trudged through snow and came alongside the bent metal that was once a beautiful Navy fighter aircraft, he could see that Jesse was in horrible pain. Despite the superb airmanship that allowed Jesse to escape a catastrophic crash and certain death, the resulting damage was not insignificant. He was pinned down in the cockpit, embraced in a death grip by what used to be his most favorite place to sit and earn his keep. It didn't help that he was also exposed to subzero winter temperatures as nightfall approached. Tom quickly extinguished the growing fires around Jesse's airplane with snow, and then made it back to his own crash site to transmit a request to the rescue helicopter to bring an axe to dislodge Jesse and also a fire extinguisher in case of new fires. He brought back gloves and a scarf to comfort and protect Jesse from the cold. With nothing else to do, Tom fervently tried to free Jesse from the wreck while simultaneously trying to provide whatever aid he could. Time was not on their side.

By the time the helicopter arrived, Jesse was fading fast. All efforts to cut away or bend the metal that was wrapped around him failed. With night closing in, Tom was forced to do the hardest thing he had ever done—leave his dying friend and wingman alone on top of an inhospitable and foreign mountain in a war zone. While Tom was explaining the plan to get more help, Jesse spoke what would end up being his final words: "Please tell Daisy I love her." Daisy was Jesse's wife. The amazing life of this pioneering Navy pilot ended thousands of miles away from where it all started in Mississippi. Thankfully, his final resting place was guarded by two Navy fighter aircraft that would forever mark the hallowed ground of extraordinary service and sacrifice. They also symbolized the nonnegotiable service contract between pilot and wingman.

Tom, the humblest gentleman I may have ever met, was quick to point out that he would have done the same for any of the other men in the squadron, and they for him. "I just happened to be the one that went in that day," he told me. "If it hadn't been me, it would have been one of the others." Jesse's remains are still on that mountain despite an attempt sixty years later to repatriate them. The organizer and leader of this expedition to bring Jesse back was none other than the consummate wingman, Tom Hudner. Unfortunately, the North Koreans don't seem to be big fans of bringing closure to our fallen heroes.

Tom earned the Medal of Honor for his selfless heroism that day, and Jesse was immortalized when they named a ship after him in 1972—the USS *Jesse L. Brown* (DE/FF/FFT-1089). And yes, Daisy received Jesse's last message from Tom.

Thankfully, the typical fighter pilot doesn't face situations like this very often. From my perspective, the payoff for unconditional and selfless service to others is joy and satisfaction. It creates a powerful emotional surge that acts like an addiction over time. When fully developed, the alternative, which is selfishness, becomes unacceptable. In aviation, it is this constant reinforcement of "troops first" and "you never leave your wingman" combined with the emotional rewards that follow when you do it right that result in the unbelievable heroism exemplified by Jesse and Tom. It permeates every decision, action, and behavior and defines who you are.

And at the end of a mission, it is not "bombs on target" that help us choose happy; it is the fulfillment of that inviolable and unwritten service contract with our wingman. And from there, it is the fulfillment of that inviolable and unwritten service contract with exposed ground troops that magnify it even more.

Kids and Service

From a parenting perspective, kids benefit tremendously from a sense of service. They are never too young to share or help. They are never too young to volunteer. I truly feel sorry for people, especially kids, who are denied the experience of service to others. Sometimes it is inconvenient. Sometimes it is potentially risky. Many times you are neither thanked nor appreciated. And often the act of service is not deserved by those receiving it. But those challenges notwithstanding, there is always a payoff when it comes to choosing happy. My kids have served meals to the homeless, boxed packages for deployed troops, volunteered at hospitals and adult care centers, and read books to children. A selfless act of kindness or service is remarkable in the sense that the emotional reward is independent of the size or scope of the act. It happens regardless. The only way to compromise the effort is to be motivated by something different than selfless service.

As I tell my kids, the moment you do something purely for yourself, whether it is for glory or recognition, you compromise the true benefits of your service to others. Many of the schools my children have attended mandate community service hours—presumably to generate an appetite for service. The intent is certainly noble but what tends to happen, with some kids anyhow, is that they treat the service opportunity more like a job or a homework assignment rather than true and genuine service to others. This subtle difference changes the entire emotional outcome. Instead of the joy and satisfaction felt when helping others for no other reason than it being the right thing to do, the experience becomes just a graduation checklist item. This also extends to the college-bound kids looking for a competitive edge for admissions. They are sometimes encouraged and influenced by parents or counselors to start a "charity" for the nefarious purpose of gaining an admissions advantage. This type of endeavor, even if it ends up helping people, offers no happiness value. It only works if the focus is completely on others and if you don't care whether anybody knows about it but yourself. Sharing or bragging about all the wonderful things you did on Facebook, Snapchat, or Twitter will quickly convert an act of goodness to an act of self-interest. When it comes to service and choosing happiness, it helps to be an anonymous and frequent donor.

> "Instead of the joy and satisfaction felt when helping others for no other reason than it being the right thing to do, the experience becomes just a graduation checklist item."

Happiness as Your Default Position

Is happiness an illusion? Is it even occasionally or accidently possible? In my opinion, if you demonstrate and guide your kids through the processes I've learned from my African villager friends, my Maasai warrior host, my career as a Navy fighter pilot, my Christian faith, and the examples of Joe Caruso, Tom Hudner, and Jesse Brown, happiness tends to become your default position. Yes, you will drift away from it from time to time when things seem to be conspiring against you, but when that happens it's like catching your balance or adjusting your eyes to the darkness; you quickly stabilize or you quickly activate your night vision. It's just a momentary inconvenience. And when you have a support team around you that embraces the same happiness approach that you do, together you can power through the darkest hours or the biggest challenges. These key happiness reinforcements often give you that special nudge or beam of light that helps you to regain your happiness state of mind.

Let's not forget about the improved success trajectory and leadership benefits of these happiness tools. When you only focus on things within your power to control and change, you simultaneously expand the range, height, and frequency of your potential success, and you are always prepared for less-desirable outcomes. You also recognize your dependence on others for big accomplishments. This helps you create a community of inspired contributions and determine the intersection of a common and noble vision for the future. If you want fully committed people on your team, ready to place their energy, focus, intellect, and faith in your hands, inspire them instead of commanding them, and teach them how to choose happiness.

★★★

 FIGHTER PILOT PARENT TAKEAWAYS—
Happiness Principles

☆ Teach children that happiness is a choice.

☆ Allow children to only obsess about what they can control, not what they can't.

☆ When children own their own energy, focus, intellect, and faith, they can change the magnitude and vector of each.

☆ Show children how to make an inventory and be grateful, thankful, and appreciative every day for the small stuff.

☆ Teach and model selfless and anonymous service to others.

☆ Remember: Your troops and wingmen come first.

CHAPTER TEN

FINAL THOUGHTS: FAITH, FAMILY, FRIENDS, AND FUN

———

I was an eighteen-year-old plebe at the naval academy on September 21, 1979—the very first official National POW/MIA Recognition Day observed at the academy—when I came face-to-face with my very first legend: Viet-Nam Prisoner of War, Paul Galanti. Commander Galanti served seven years as a North Vietnamese POW after being shot down in his A-4 Skyhawk. He suffered being drugged, deprived of sleep, and made to sit on a small stool in an unheated interrogation room for ten days and nights during the coldest part of the year. He was forced to apologize to the camp commander for an inexcusable infraction— sharing Life Savers candies with a fellow prisoner. Up to that point, I had been feeling sorry for myself for having to "persevere" through the hardships of plebe year. How embarrassing.

A month earlier, during our plebe summer, we had begun to develop a reverence for these special heroes, and we started using their extraordinary survival and resistance techniques—in the event we would ever find ourselves in circumstances like theirs in what seemed to be a very distant future. My first reaction when I met this Navy fighter pilot legend was surprise. He was categorically normal. I don't know what I was expecting, but it certainly wasn't a normal guy who was smiling, joking, and fun. He truly loved life. The surprises continued. After he showed us the prison possessions he was "allowed" to bring back from captivity (black pajamas and a small rice bowl), I listened in disbelief as he actually said he was thankful for the experience. How could that be? He had been deprived of everything—freedom, liberty, basic human dignity, basic human rights, contact with his family, contact with his friends, contact with his fellow prisoners of war—for almost seven years. Oh, and did I mention that he was tortured? He explained that his nearly seven years of captivity could be summed up in the space of a postage stamp, but he learned a valuable lesson in appreciation.

From that moment on, my path would quickly lead to a future that potentially included the same day of destiny Commander Galanti unexpectedly found himself in on June 17, 1966, the day he was captured. I often wondered if I had what it took to be able to endure what he did and come out the other side with my dignity, my honor, and my positive attitude still intact. Unlike previous wars, where most POWs were enlisted ground troops, North Vietnamese prisoner of war camps were full of US Navy, Air Force, and Marine airmen who were mostly officers. Surface-to-air missiles and air-to-air missiles had replaced bullets and artillery. The sky had become much more dangerous. The total number of repatriated POWs included 325 Air Force personnel, 138 Navy personnel, and 26 Marines. It seemed to me at the time that I needed to contemplate the very distinct possibility of captivity in my future service.

My preparation started with memorizing the Code of Conduct, which is a brief guide from the US Department of Defense on how a service member is to behave if taken into captivity.

The Code of the US Fighting Force

Article I: I am an American, fighting in the forces which guard my country and our way of life. I am prepared to give my life in their defense.

Article II: I will never surrender of my own free will. If in command, I will never surrender the members of my command while they still have the means to resist.

Article III: If I am captured I will continue to resist by all means available. I will make every effort to escape and aid others to escape. I will accept neither parole nor special favors from the enemy.

Article IV: If I become a prisoner of war, I will keep faith with my fellow prisoners. I will give no information or take part in any action which might be harmful to my comrades. If I am senior, I will take command. If not, I will obey the lawful orders of those appointed over me and will back them up in every way.

Article V: When questioned, should I become a prisoner of war, I am required to give name, rank, service number, and date of birth. I will evade answering further questions to the utmost of my ability. I will make no oral or written statements disloyal to my country and its allies or harmful to their cause.

Article VI: I will never forget that I am an American, fighting for freedom, responsible for my actions, and dedicated to the principles which made my country free. I will trust in my God and in the United States of America.

After hearing story after story from former POWs and the circumstances they had to deal with, many of us, I'm sure, had doubts about our ability live up to the code. And thankfully never having had to experience that situation during my career, I am still left wondering if I would have had what it takes. Although I didn't obsess too much over it, the thought of ejecting over enemy territory, becoming a prisoner of war, and being deprived of every human right took on a much more serious meaning as I advanced along my fighter pilot career path.

As the potential for sudden and complete loss of freedom, liberty, human dignity, and human rights started to become more than just an abstract concept, the value that those concepts represented grew exponentially for me. On service selection night, an event where naval academy seniors choose their future career, I anxiously and proudly chose aviation—albeit with my celebratory mood slightly dampened by the sobering reality of what potentially might lie ahead. It was starting to become real.

Following graduation in June of 1982, as I was driving my Toyota pickup through the main gate of Naval Air Station Pensacola, Florida, a flight of four A-4 Skyhawks, just like Commander Galanti's, flew directly overhead in tight formation. As I watched in amazement, I quickly concluded that my life was about to radically change. And as I imagined the long journey ahead and the list of possible things that could go wrong, that moment of raw emotional exhilaration and excitement was quickly replaced by trepidation and the feeling of smallness. The first real step into the unknown always feels like that, doesn't it? For me, of course, each step along my chosen career path simultaneously led me closer to something I started to consider

> **"When you truly consider the loss of something you should cherish above all other benefits, its value continues to rise."**

worse than death, the complete and sudden loss of all those things that most Americans take for granted: freedom and liberty. When you truly consider the loss of something you should cherish above all other benefits, its value continues to rise.

As I advanced through each phase of flight school, just as the 138 Navy prisoners of war before me did, I began to consider a potential outcome that was even worse than both death and the loss of freedom: failing to keep faith with and serve my fellow wingmen, especially if we found ourselves in an enemy prison camp. After all, we now truly considered ourselves American fighting men and women, guarding our freedom and way of life, dedicated to the principles which made our country free, and dependent on one another for survival—in the air, of course, but also and especially in captivity. It became clear that the "troops first" and "never leave your wingman behind" mantras were the real distinguishing themes in every stunning Viet-Nam prisoner of war survival story. The nature and demands of our very profession were simultaneously preparing us for the extreme possibility of sudden and complete loss of freedom.

Gaining Confidence for the Future

I did start to gain confidence in my ability to perform like those 138 legacy Navy POW aviators before me. I knew that in our shared culture, we were subconsciously preparing for it every day, and through many combat missions, I never really thought about getting shot down too much other than during our normal preflight preparation routine. I knew we were being trained to be really good at what we did.

Much later in my career I met distinguished prisoners of war such as Admiral James Stockdale and Senator John McCain. Their examples of "troops first" and "never leave your wingman behind" are extraordinary and widely known. But it wasn't until I participated in the commissioning of the USS *Stockdale* in 2009 that I had the unique and life-changing privilege of engaging on a personal level with both POWs and Medal of Honor winners alike—this time as a fellow combat veteran. I listened to their stories. I asked questions. They asked me lots of questions. They were humble, and I was in awe. Most striking to me was that they were extraordinarily ordinary Americans. There was no way you could tell that they had spent several years of their young lives surviving an ordeal that few could ever contemplate. Not only did they find ways to cope and support one another, but they actually thrived in some cases. It was during this period that I met and became friends with Charlie Plumb and Leo Thorsness.

Charlie was a Navy fighter pilot and Leo was an Air Force fighter pilot. Charlie flew F-4 Phantoms and Leo flew F-105 Thunderchiefs. Charlie would become the chaplain of the "Hanoi Hilton" (the infamous North Vietnamese prison camp). Leo would learn from future POWs that he had been awarded the Medal of Honor for his heroic actions during a mission he flew only eleven days prior to being shot down. Like Tom Hudner, his total disregard for personal safety and his extraordinary bravery and courage under enemy fire leaped from his Medal of Honor citation, a secret document that was not disclosed until after he was repatriated to prevent his captors from making an example out of him. Charlie would go on to become a professional public speaker.

He mesmerized us during the USS *Stockdale* commissioning week with his powerful story. His polished pitch included the main theme that attitude (choosing happiness) is the key to survival. Leo passed in 2017, and when he did, Senator McCain, a fellow prisoner of war, made the following statement: "Colonel Thorsness endured unspeakable pain and suffering because of his steadfast adherence to our code of conduct during his six years in captivity, including a year in solitary confinement. But Leo never let this experience break his spirit and inspired the rest of us with his patriotism, perseverance, and hope that we would someday be free."

For years, Leo and Charlie faced a nightmarish existence of degradation, loneliness, boredom, hunger, and pain, mostly alone, and confined to a seven-by-seven-foot cell. Their only source of support and comfort was through communication with each other, a strong belief in their code of conduct, and the inspirational values that their country stood for.

Two Heroes

Communication was not simple in captivity. It was a forbidden and punishable offense, but this is where POWs exceled in fulfillment of their code of conduct duty: resistance. As each POW arrived in prison, each was taught by fellow prisoners a simple communication tool based on the conversion of letters to numbers. They broke the alphabet into a five-letter by five-letter grid, excluding the letter "K" which could be covered by "C." To communicate, they would "tap" a letter based on its sequence on the grid. For example, letter "A" would be a "tap," pause, then another "tap." Letter "Z" would be "tap-tap-tap-tap-tap," pause, then "tap-tap-tap-tap-tap." It took some getting used to, but it was simple, fairly discreet, very useful, and could cover a very large distance if you tapped hard enough. You could even blink it if you needed to.

The POWs used this tool for everything. They told stories, shared news updates, held classes, debriefed torture sessions, plotted resistance techniques and tactics, comforted each other, prayed, and paid tribute to their country—a country that, despite its issues and growing pains, represented the best and most virtuous approach to governing free people.

Their love for and devotion to their country intensified in captivity as their daily experience, the polar opposite in the extreme, reinforced their belief in the core ideals, principles, and values that made the United States so special despite its flaws. And their flag, symbolic of both their country's exceptionalism as well as its imperfection, served to unify them in their resistance.

Some years ago, I was part of an organizing team that brought both Charlie and Leo together for a private event, where we gathered one night at the Ronald Reagan Presidential Library to hear them do what they do best—share important lessons from their experience and help people apply those lessons in their daily lives and in business. As I've seen before in other venues, the room was entranced as these two American heroes and legends recounted the extraordinary environment they suddenly found themselves in as young men, the different phases of their captivity, and the special moments that gave them the strength they needed to persevere—just when they thought they had nothing left. But this time, they were on stage together, which added an interesting dynamic to their normal solo performances.

There was the normal Navy versus Air Force ribbing, of course, but the real fascination was how they both had synchronized their will and their attitude in defiance of their captors and what they stood for. They took great delight in both their successful as well as unsuccessful attempts at resistance, and they seemed to have taken turns either receiving or drawing much-needed strength from each other and others through their rudimentary communication system. At the end of this once-in-a-lifetime experience and returning full circle to my first encounter with Commander Galanti as a plebe at the naval academy, I sheepishly joined them on stage as part of a panel discussion on how their legacy and leadership inspired future generations of fighter pilots; how precious freedom and liberty truly are; and how important it is for those who enjoy those benefits to never take them for granted and to defend both at all costs.

After I gushed profusely in an attempt to convey how all fighter pilots, past and present, felt about them and their courageous example, Leo and Charlie shared the story of Mike Christian and his flag—a story that got national attention when then-Washington State Senator Leo shared it from the house floor during discussion about a resolution concerning flag desecration.

The Rag in the Gutter That Became a Flag

Charlie and Leo told the audience at the library that in their final year of captivity, the rules had relaxed slightly and they were briefly allowed outside for some rare personal hygiene. As their large, filthy POW group gathered around a concrete water tank, they took turns pouring water from a bucket over their heads, while the guards encircled them. After a while the guards would generally become either too disinterested or distracted by their duties to maintain a constant watch over each POW.

Alongside the tank, there was a drainage gutter that funneled runoff away from the tank out under the prison wall, which led the water to freedom on the other side. By that time, all the POWs were masters of quickly recognizing and exploiting any opportunity for resistance. Mike Christian spotted a nasty-looking discarded rag in the gutter near the small opening in the wall, and from this ratty rag he planned to produce an American flag—a singular objective that was shared by all his POW colleagues. The ingenuity and persistence they applied to this premier act of defiance knew no bounds and defined the phrase "necessity is the mother of invention."

Their oppressors and captors, the delegates of the enemies of freedom everywhere, clearly recognized the unifying power of their rectangular symbol of freedom, liberty, sacrifice, and the commitment to constantly improve, serve, and protect those freedoms. They also knew that it registered a primary threat to their oppressive political system because the principles the US flag inherently promoted could potentially sow the seeds of future dissension and revolution.

So in recognition of that threat, the enemy reserved a special level of punishment for the possession of any facsimile of a US flag, no matter how imperfect or tattered. If one was discovered, punishment was swift and brutal. Each POW understood the risk, yet harsh punishment notwithstanding, they were undeterred in their quest to manufacture flags from anything they could find. From rough prison "toilet paper" to rare patches of cloth, they were constantly fashioning a flag from something. When production of a new flag was complete, the owner would officially activate his flag through discreet announcement and then, with great pride and satisfaction, present the flag while the entire camp rendered appropriate honors in an official but discreet ceremony. Fully appraising all this risk and reward, Mike did not hesitate.

In Leo's retelling of the story, he said that Mike whispered to him that he saw something in the gutter that he wanted to get back to his cell without attracting the guard's attention. Leo, quickly adapting without knowing Mike's exact intentions, started talking loudly to draw attention away from Mike's object of interest so he could secretly pick it up and shield it from view as he concealed it in his pajamas. Phase one of his plan complete, Mike returned to his cell and examined his prize. It was a small, dirt-saturated handkerchief that may have been white at one time. On to phase two—making it white.

Leo and Charlie explained to the audience that soap was hard to come by at camp so it was a precious commodity. The POWs shared their small treasures equally, and when they found out what Mike had in mind, they graciously contributed their precious soap pieces to the project and looked forward to the unveiling ceremony. Mike went right to work and began the laborious process of bringing his sewer hanky back to life. By prison standards, dull gray was the equivalent of bright white, and so, after a rigorous scrubbing, phase two was successfully completed. On to phase three.

In every POW movie I've ever seen, there is always one guy that can scrounge up anything. In the Hanoi Hilton, I guess Mike competed for that title. Fully committed to project completion, he found and concealed a piece of red tile that he ground into a fine dust powder. After he mixed it with a little water, he created a maroon die (prison standard for red) that he could fashion into stripes. Completing phase three, it was now on to blue and the stars.

The last color was a little more challenging. It was hard to come by anything that was blueish, but fortunately, Leo and Charlie had a very small supply of some unknown medication; it just happened to be a blue pill. (This pill must have held some miraculous and mystical healing power since it was prescribed for all ailments.) A decision was made to forego a small portion of this miracle drug so Mike could finish the project. Delicately transferring the color from the pill to a square corner of the sewer hanky, Mike completed phase four of his project, assisted as usual by all of his wingmen. Now for the finale: a star (prison standard for fifty stars).

The star was a little easier. Bamboo wood shards were plentiful and easy to convert into a respectable needle. Every piece of cloth they owned (pajamas and a blanket) was always frayed and constantly "leaking" star-quality thread. With a single thread from his blanket,

Mike stitched a high-quality star onto his field of blue and completed his beautiful prison flag, fully knowing he would eventually be caught. The question was when. By now, he was at the two-week mark, an eternity considering the scrutiny and oversight dedicated to finding any and all reasons to punish the POWs. He worked with stealth at night under his mosquito net, so far unbeknownst to the guards. The POWs all felt a surprise inspection was overdue and it wouldn't be long before the guards would strip them down, bring them outside, and go through everything in their cell, eventually finding Mike's flag.

With the odds of detection building with each phase of the project, Mike knew he had to act as soon as he was finished. Early one morning, before too many guards were active, Mike got up, held up the flag, and waved it for all to see, including any guards if they were looking. The POWs came to attention and saluted, Leo told our audience. Some of them even began to cry, he said, choking up himself in the retelling. For the record, everyone in the Reagan Library was crying too—forty-five years later.

As expected, Mike's flag was found that night, and he was taken to the torture cell. When he was returned, Leo said, again choking up, Mike was badly beaten. He was bloody and semiconscious and so badly hurt that even his voice was gone. But Mike was a tough man. In a couple of weeks, he had recovered and immediately started looking for another piece of cloth.

The Symbol of Freedom and the Sacred Bond

I don't think anyone who has heard or read that story could ever look at the American flag in the same way again. I don't think anyone who has heard or read that story would ever feel comfortable kneeling, sitting, or talking through the national anthem, or failing to respect the flag when it is officially honored at public events. Yet ironically, the most globally recognized symbol of freedom, liberty, human rights, opportunity, and the commitment to the preservation of those ideals has become the object of protest for some professional athletes in pursuit of those very same principles. It makes no sense—it's almost like promoting good hygiene by not bathing. The flag readily acknowledges the imperfections of our government while simultaneously honoring the service and sacrifice of those who have committed to continuously improving it throughout its history, forever guided by a universally accepted set of inspirational values.

I ask myself how the POWs I've encountered would respond to this protest trend among professional athletes. I think first, as Americans, they would automatically get behind any American who was legitimately oppressed or denied any basic human right, no matter how slight. That would be a nonnegotiable. I also think they would support any nonviolent First Amendment activity for any American, even if the basis for their grievance was unclear or unwarranted. That would be a nonnegotiable as well. But when it comes to disrespecting the one symbol of hope and opportunity that they have pledged a sacred oath to support and defend, I'm pretty sure they would respectfully decline, while also acknowledging another person's right to do so. But the next part would be a little more challenging for them, as it was for Pittsburgh Steeler offensive lineman Alejandro Villanueva, who stood alone during a pregame national anthem ceremony while his teammates waited in the tunnel.

Captain Villanueva, a military academy graduate, had earlier served as an Army Ranger in Afghanistan. He was the real deal, with a Bronze Star to show for it. He was cut from the same cloth as Charlie, Leo, and every other POW and fighter pilot I know. On game day, however, he was unfortunately asked to do something he clearly agonized over. Any one of us would have probably felt the same way. He was presented with two mutually exclusive actions of equal value: his love for his country and the ideals represented by our flag or his love for his teammates—the wingmen he served and supported. No matter how he went, it was going to hurt.

Although he chose the flag that Sunday, the very next day he was still agonizing over his choice, since he had also dedicated himself to the service and support of his teammates. I felt horrible for him, and he certainly has nothing to apologize for. His situation was one that POWs found themselves in every moment of captivity. They were notorious for refusing special privileges and extra comforts so they could maintain solidarity and fellowship with their teammates. And they would hold that line up until the point when they risked being disloyal to their country or faced imminent death. And even when they made the right choice, like Captain Villanueva did, in my opinion, they still agonized over it because they felt as though they had broken a sacred bond with their wingmen. Unconditional service to others will do that, but good teammates and wingmen understand such gut-wrenching choices, and they will still accept you and welcome you back to fight another day. Charlie and Leo's enemy constantly tried to drive a wedge between each man, and between each man and his country, through torture, privilege, and deception. They underestimated the power of selfless service to others and the inspiration that American ideals could generate.

It was not uncommon for POWs to bend and occasionally break under the physical and mental stress they were subjected to. One by one, each of them would fail at some point. But one by one, each of them would be emotionally resuscitated and rejuvenated from the grief and despair over their perceived infidelity to their team, their country, or their code of conduct. Every night they closed their endless twenty-four-hour cycle of hell with a recommitment ceremony to their wingmen, their country, their faith, their families, and their code of conduct.

Charlie described this ritual for us that night in the Reagan Library as our special night came to a close. As the guards retired to their night positions and a subdued posture, the POWs exploited their relative peace and safety to renew their devotion to the fight they knew they would have to wage and win the next day. I can't remember who Charlie said would start it, but they all would join, in their own special Hanoi Hilton fashion, with all their military brothers and sisters across the globe who would be retiring their own individual units' American flag in a ceremony called "colors," signifying the official end of the duty day. On military bases everywhere, the bugle call "Taps" synchronizes the various unit flag retreats. Moving cars come to a stop, people outdoors stop whatever they are doing and stand at attention, and those in uniform render a salute. This ceremony happens every day around the world, and the POWs were not going to break faith with their fellow service members just because of the inconvenience of captivity.

Ironically, they would start the "Taps" ceremony with their tap code. Every POW, even those who were hobbled and bedridden from either recent torture or illness, would attempt to stand and salute whatever makeshift flag Mike Christian, or some other aspiring flag maker, had fabricated that day. They did this so often that the rhythm, pace, and distinctive patterns of a tapped Pledge of Allegiance sounded like a familiar and beloved song. As Charlie was explaining this procedure to us, he admitted that many of the words and phrases were reduced to shorthand to enhance the speed of communication. Charlie explained that at the end of the daily "Taps" ceremony, someone would close it with the following tap sequence: tap-tap, pause, tap-tap, tap, pause, tap-tap, and tap, pause, tap.

For you novice tap code readers, the letters are G-B-A—more commonly known as God Bless America.

★★★

Why You Shouldn't Say, "I Just Want Them to Be Happy"

I often think of the daily POW "Taps" event and the interesting correlation to parenting. Each day there are ups, downs, celebrations, disappointments, setbacks, and advancements. But each night, you put those things to rest, reaffirm your unconditional love for those you care most about, recharge the power and strength within your control, and rediscover those small things for which you are grateful. In our house, this took the form of prayer time as we tucked our kids in.

I wrote this book because I know that, even though I may routinely fail at being the best parent I can be, if I don't strive for excellence, I won't be anywhere near as good as I want to be.

The life lessons that I learned in my evolution as a fighter pilot are the very same lessons and wisdom that guided me as a parent. And although the lessons I share in this book are not unique to fighter pilots or any other professionals expected to perform at a high level and at great personal risk, the alternative options that were available to us have already been tried and rejected by the harsh world of reality. Our system was truly written in blood and perfected over time.

As the proud parent of four kids, whose ages span fourteen years, I've seen every trend in parenting over the past thirty years. During this period of rapidly changing culture, technology, and values, there is still no better system of binding people to a higher set of principles, performance, true happiness, and achievement than a system that has figured how to take ordinary people like me and teach them how to do seemingly extraordinary things. Why would I chance the number one priority in life—my children—to anything less?

This book was written out of love for kids and those who want the best for them. Parenting is not a checklist or guidebook. The rules change every day and at every age. It comes down to a set of guidelines and a set of defining nonnegotiable principles that allow you to genuinely and authentically lead your children through every predictable and unpredictable challenge and opportunity they face in life. Just as with music scales, there is a fixed set of whole and half notes, but from that basic foundation, you can write an infinite number of songs. My suggestion is to use this book to help your children write their own symphony.

And finally, never be the parent who, when asked what they want their child to be in the future, says, "I just want them to be happy." This annoys me to no end because it implies that these parents have no control or power in their child's development and trajectory. The fighter pilot parent would say instead, "I want to help my children discover what they are passionate about and support them in developing that passion with their dignity, character, and integrity intact. They will be happy if I do my job right."

Before our magical Reagan Library event came to a close, Charlie and Leo answered one more question. Someone in the audience revisited the tap code and prison communications topic. I had never considered the question they asked, but I became very interested in the answer. Before you read Charlie and Leo's response, consider your own experience and then answer the question they were asked: "What were the most common things you would talk about?"

Charlie and Leo looked at each other and smiled. And then, almost as if they had rehearsed it, they turned back to the audience and boldly stated in unison, "Faith, family, friends, and fun." When all else is taken from you, these are the precious gifts that conspire to replenish your strength, reinforce your will, and give you the means to overcome.

★★★

Go be a Fighter Pilot Parent.
G-B-Y and G-B-A.
God bless you.
And God bless America.

ABOUT THE AUTHOR

It is surprising, given that Brick Conners didn't have the opportunity to see the ocean or to fly in a jet until the age of seventeen, that his path from his humble terrestial prison in upstate New York ultimately led to a career that spanned twenty-seven years of nonstop sea and air work—all from the vantage point of an F/A-18 Hornet cockpit.

The catalyst to his destiny was a deep passion for the original American sport of lacrosse, combined with a strong desire to serve. Fortunately, the US Naval Academy was willing to partner in both areas and became his alma mater in 1982.

In a career that was 99 percent pure exhilarating fun balanced with 1 percent pure terror, the lessons of leadership, survival, faith, love, perseverance, and camaraderie were plentiful and direct, and they changed his life. As a Navy Strike Fighter, Brick amassed over 4,500 hours and nearly 1,000 arrested carrier landings during multiple combat deployments. His tours of duty included F/A-18 Hornet Squadron Command. He also provided leadership and instruction to two of the Navy's elite air power training organizations, the Naval Strike and Air Warfare Center and Naval Strike Force Training Pacific. In the blink of an eye, it was over, and he bid farewell to his beloved Navy at his final command—Naval Base Ventura County.

Driven to enhance his business acumen, Brick embarked on a second career as an executive with Booz Allen Hamilton Inc. and then with Northrop Grumman Aerospace, where he returned to his aviation roots as he supported both US and international tactical aircraft sales and provided design strategies for the aircraft of the future. Capitalizing on those rewarding professional experiences and powered by a brand-new MBA, Brick began partnering with other companies as a professional trajectory enhancer—otherwise known as a business and leadership consultant. From finance to transportation, the lessons and experience from his unique past continue to be useful to others.

But if given the choice, Brick's go-to move would be to coach and mentor young men and women—either professionally or through his first passion, lacrosse. And when it comes to joy and fulfillment, there is no greater force in his life than the support from, and pride in, his devoted family—his wife, Terrie, and their four children, Sarah, Rachel, Anna, and Bradford.